About the Author

Dr. David Noble has served as a pastor and staff member in rural, small town and urban congregations. David also has worked several years in university and healthcare administration. He currently serves as a pastor, consultant, adjunct professor, and chaplain.

David has received degrees from Truman State University, the University of North Texas, Princeton Theological Seminary, and Midwestern Baptist Theological Seminary. His doctoral studies concentrated on equipping church leaders to guide their congregations through conflict.

David is the founder of Building Healthy Churches® and serves as a workshop leader and consultant in the areas of biblical conflict resolution and church health.

Church Conflict by the Book

David C. Noble

BHC Publishing
Kansas City, Missouri

Church Conflict by the Book

Copyright © 2013 by David C. Noble

All rights reserved.

Originally published as
Winning the Real Battle at Church:
Safeguard Your Congregation Against Destructive Conflict

Published by BHC Publishing, Box 482296, Kansas City, Missouri 64148

ISBN 978-0-615-63958-1

Printed in the United States of America

Additional copies of this book and its
group discussion guide can be purchased at

www.churchconflictbythebook.com

Table of Contents

Introduction 1

1. Why Can't We Get Along?

    The War Around Us 4

    The War Within Us 8

    The War Among Us 13

    Devil Talk 17

    Conflict from God's Perspective 21

2. When Two or Three Disagree

    Motives Matter 25

    Confront Sin 30

    Offer Grace 36

    Grow Up in Christ 40

    Preserve the Precious Gift of Unity 44

3. Trouble at the Top

    Seeds of Sedition 48

    The Fruit of Rebellion 52

    Preemptive Strike 58

    Leadership or Abuse? 63

    Parting Company 70

4. Rebellion in the Ranks

    Choose a New Leader 76

    Wolves Among You 81

The Spirit of Jezebel 87

The Care and Feeding of Troublemakers 94

On Sheep and Shepherding 101

5. Matters of the Heart

Sweet Surrender 105

Submit from the Heart 110

Win the Enemy, Not the Fight 117

Seek Wisdom from Above 122

Trust God 126

6. The Ways of a Peacemaker

Glorify God 132

Focus on Christ 139

Speak the Truth in Love 145

Walk in the Spirit 156

Remain Steadfast 163

Scriptures for Resolving Conflict 170

Using this Resource in Your Church 181

Endnotes 184

Introduction

Drive by First Friendly Church[1] and you'll see an impressive, beautiful facility. The lawn is manicured immaculately. A state-of-the-art electronic sign welcomes guests and displays an impressive array of activities. Next to the sign stands a recently constructed family life center. Everything indicates that the church is growing and that there is something for everyone inside its doors. However, First Friendly Church is anything but friendly.

Worship services are strained and attendance is falling. Warm smiles and hugs have been replaced by suspicious glances and hurt feelings. Accusation permeates committee and business meetings. Church finances are reeling. Members offer limp, half-hearted handshakes to guests, wondering why anyone would visit their church.

First Friendly Church is anything but friendly. It's a war zone!

Is your church like First Friendly Church? Since you're reading this book, there's a strong possibility that you are in the middle of a church conflict or trying to recover from one. Even if everything is peaceful in your congregation, now is the best time to prepare for the future. Conflict is inevitable, but it doesn't have to tear your church apart. It is an opportunity for you and your church to grow spiritually and unleash the transforming power of God's Word.

Church Conflict by the Book will take you on a journey that will introduce you to the spiritual realities behind church conflict, equip you to respond to conflict biblically, and teach you how to open the doors to peace by ushering God's presence into your church. You will discover new ways of seeing and responding to personality clashes, conflicting priorities, and struggles for control.

Is this book right for you? Absolutely! Since conflict is inevitable, every Christian who is concerned about the health and effectiveness of his or her church should read *Church Conflict by the Book*. Though you may not hold a formal position of church leadership, God is calling you to use your influence to build up your church. Other people listen to you and follow your example. You can use your influence to damage or strengthen your congregation.

Your godly, Spirit-filled example can grow in its influence, ultimately affecting your entire congregation. Believe the promise of Philippians 2:14-15, "Do everything without complaining or arguing, so that you may become blameless and pure, children of God without fault in a crooked and depraved generation, in which you shine like stars in the universe."[2]   My prayer is that your life will shine for Christ in your congregation!

I urge you to read through this book carefully and slowly. Don't skim through it, seeking to justify your point of view or discover a "quick fix" for your church conflict. Allow God's Word to work in your heart. Invite others in your congregation to join you in reading this book. You can meet together as a small group on a weekly basis and use this book with the free study guide that is available at www.churchconflictbythebook.com. Plan to meet together weekly to pray for your church and discuss how God is changing each of you.

Victory in spiritual warfare is costly and rarely easy, but the peace that comes with victory is worth your sacrifice and personal involvement. You will find a sweet reward as you see God's Word alive and active in your circumstances. You'll be changed as you prayerfully read, meditate and apply God's Word in your life. As God changes you, He will use you to transform your congregation, enabling it to become the beautiful bride for which Christ died:

...Christ loved the church and gave himself up
for her to make her holy, cleansing her by the
washing with water through the word, and to
present her to himself as a radiant church,
without stain or wrinkle or any other blemish,
but holy and blameless (Ephesians 5:26-27).

Keeping Christ's church stain-free and wrinkle-free
takes effort from every member, even in peaceful times.
Maintaining the unity and peace Christ bestows on the
church requires diligence and work. We cannot afford to
let our guard down when a climate of peace prevails. This
book will offer every church member instruction in
specific ways to maintain unity and peace.

I know what it's like to experience church conflict. I
also know that regardless of how dark and hopeless your
situation might seem, peace is possible. No matter how hot
the flames of conflict might burn, beauty can rise from the
ashes. In the meantime, in the midst of the conflict, guard
your heart. Keep it pure. Keep it focused on Christ.

David C. Noble

Why Can't We Get Along?

Have you wondered why we experience so much conflict in our churches? We should be able to get along with one another. After all, we are brothers and sisters in Christ, filled with the Spirit of God and called to live in newness of life. We enjoy "every spiritual blessing in Christ" (Ephesians 1:3). Despite these realities, destructive conflict continues to damage far too many of our congregations. The Bible tells us why - we're in the middle of a spiritual battle!

This chapter will help you understand Satan's tactics against believers and experience victory in the midst of church conflict. Other Christians are not our enemies; the Bible clearly indicates that the Devil is our real adversary. Spiritual battles must be fought using spiritual means. So let's look to God's Word and put on the full armor of God so that our churches can stand firm against the Devil's schemes!

The War Around Us

Nearly every American was touched by the harsh realities of World War II. Rationing affected almost every household. News from the front lines made daily headlines. Everyone knew someone who was serving in the armed forces and many people had lost loved ones. Despite these hardships, very few Americans questioned the war. They knew the danger was real. They believed that victory was worth the sacrifice, however dear and costly.

Today the average American is detached from the experience of war. Life seems to go on as normal no matter what happens on battlefields around the world. Politicians openly question the justification for fighting. Public opinion is divided, not united.

Given these dramatic changes in how the average American experiences war, it's not surprising that many Christians and churches disregard the reality of spiritual warfare. It seems removed from their daily experience. Rather than address what is facing their families and churches, they choose to continue blissfully from one Sunday to the next, leaving themselves unprepared for Satan's inevitable onslaught.

This approach to the Christian life ignores the Bible's clear call to be alert to spiritual warfare. The Apostle Peter warns, "Be self-controlled and alert. Your enemy the devil prowls around like a roaring lion looking for someone to devour" (1 Peter 5:8), and the Apostle Paul admonishes, "Put on the full armor of God so that you can stand your stand against the devil's schemes. For our struggle is not against flesh and blood, but against the rulers, against the authorities, against the powers of this dark world and against the spiritual forces of evil in the heavenly realms" (Ephesians 6:11-12).

We're at War!

We're at war, whether we like it or not. Satan is preoccupied with our destruction. If we fail to grasp the reality of spiritual warfare, we will be unguarded when he attacks. Our enemy is a real enemy and he has a battle plan for the demise of the church and every believer. Spiritual warfare – the battle of Satan and his demons against God and His children – will be waged until Satan is finally banished. We must be alert to this reality and be prepared to stand firm against enemy attacks.

If you're prone to underestimate Satan's power, consider what he did in biblical times. Satan destroyed Job's health, family, and possessions (Job 1:1-22), incited

David to rely on military power (1 Chronicles 21); tempted Jesus three times (Luke 4:1-13), influenced Peter to rebuke Jesus (Mark 8:31-33), entered Judas prior to his betrayal of Jesus (Luke 22:3-6), and prompted Ananias to lie to the Holy Spirit (Acts 5:1-11). And what Satan didn't accomplish personally he achieved through his demons who afflicted their victims with physical, emotional, and behavioral disorders (Matthew 9:33; Matthew 17:14-18; Luke 8:27-33).

There is no reason to believe that Satan has changed his tactics. In Ephesians 6:11, the Greek New Testament describes Satan's schemes by using the word *methodeais*, from which we get our English word "methods." Beginning with Eve in the Garden of Eden and continuing to this very

> Satan is your avowed enemy, waiting for just the right time and place to attack you.

moment, Satan uses the same methods to deceive people by leading them to question God's Word and appealing to their sinful desires. Satan is deceptive. However, he is not at all innovative so we can learn to detect his strategies.

Satan is your avowed enemy, waiting for just the right time and place to attack you. He has declared war on you and your church. However, God is sovereign over Satan and limits what he can do (Job 1:12; Luke 22:31-32). Satan cannot destroy you or Christ's Church, but he can render you and your congregation spiritually ineffective by inciting sinful attitudes and actions that destroy your testimony and your unity in Christ (John 17:20-23).

Take a few moments to reflect on the ways that Satan's "fingerprints" have been evident in the churches you've attended. Joylessness, anger, selfishness, gossip, jealously, accusation, divisiveness, impurity, and deceit are clear indicators of his demonic presence. Satan's schemes can be subtle or obvious as he attacks the Body of Christ.

Satan is a Defeated Adversary

Satan is at war with you. He stirs up ungodly actions and attitudes in an attempt to weaken or destroy the witness of individual Christians and entire congregations. However, the Bible clearly tells us that Satan is a defeated foe! Colossians 2:15 describes how God has triumphed over Satan's evil forces through the cross of Jesus Christ. This verse uses the vivid imagery of a Roman general leading his captives victoriously through the streets of Rome, publicly humiliating them as the spoils of war.

> And having disarmed the powers and authorities, he made a public spectacle of them, triumphing over them by the cross.
> *Colossians 2:15*

This is what God has done to Satan and his demons. He has defeated them through Jesus Christ, publicly and completely, and He wants to share His victory with us. When Satan prowls around looking to attack a weak area in us or our church, God calls us to believe His Word and claim Christ's victory over Satan. He calls us to stand under the shelter of the cross, allowing Christ's victory over Satan to become our victory in the present moment, in the middle of the attack.

As a fully devoted follower of Christ, put on the fighting equipment God has given you – the belt of truth, breastplate of righteousness, shoes of readiness, shield of faith, helmet of salvation, and sword of the Spirit, which is God's Word (Ephesians 6:14-17). Know that the weapons you "fight with are not the weapons of the world. On the contrary, they have divine power to demolish strongholds" (2 Corinthians 10:4). Find hope and courage in the fact that no matter how severe Satan's attacks might seem, he is powerless against the armor of God. Not only that, you know the outcome of the war!

> And the devil…was thrown into the lake of burning sulfur, where the beast and the false prophet had been thrown. They will be tormented day and night for ever and ever (Revelation 20:10).

If we understand how to use the spiritual weapons God provides, we are fully readied and protected from the enemy's onslaught. If we are prepared to use them mentally and spiritually, we can conquer anything that sets itself against God and His children.

There's a war going on around us, 24 hours a day, 365 days a year – a war that will continue until Satan is completely vanquished. Be realistic and believe God's Word. Be sober and alert. Put on the full armor of God. Allow Christ's victory over Satan to be your victory over Satan, moment by moment, day by day.

> The God of peace will soon crush Satan under your feet. The grace of our Lord Jesus be with you (Romans 16:20).

The War Within Us

There's a reason why the war around us frequently becomes a war within our churches. Satan knows that if we open ourselves to his influence, he can get us to act like unbelievers and wreak havoc in our lives and churches (Ephesians 4:27). Don't give him the opportunity!

In Acts 2:41-47 we read how the early church experienced tremendous blessings following the coming of the Holy Spirit at Pentecost. The church grew exponentially as believers "devoted themselves to the apostles' teaching and to the fellowship, to the breaking of bread and to prayer" (Acts 2:42).

However, it was not long until human sinfulness marred the fellowship and unity of the Jerusalem church. Acts 5:1-11 describes how a married couple, Ananias and Sapphira, sold a piece of property and claimed that they had given all of the proceeds to the church. They had, in fact, kept some of the money for themselves, intentionally misrepresenting their giving to God. Not long afterward, a churchwide conflict erupted between Greek-speaking and Aramaic-speaking believers (Acts 6:1-7). A complaint arose because needy widows from the minority Greek-speaking group were being overlooked during the daily distribution of food.

These problems were resolved but not before human sinfulness had created short-term disruptions in the fellowship and unity of the Jerusalem congregation. Several years later more strife broke out among the Jewish Christians who were "scattered among the nations" (James 1:1). James wrote them and asked, "What causes fights and quarrels among you?" (James 4:1a) Note his use of the plural words "fights" and "quarrels," suggesting the presence of several conflicts in congregations throughout the Roman Empire.

Ungodly Desires

James answered his question straightforwardly: "Don't they come from your desires that battle within you?" (James 4:1b) The word "desires" refers to the deliberate choice of "worldly pleasures that are contrary to the expressed will of God."[3] These desires don't represent actual needs. They are merely intense wants – wants which eventually become demands, then deteriorate into sinful attitudes and actions. Earlier in his epistle James described the outcome of this downward spiral by writing, "each one is tempted when, by his own evil desire, he is dragged away and enticed. Then, after desire has conceived, it gives birth to sin; and sin, when it is full-grown, gives birth to death" (James 1:14-15).

Satan cannot force us to sin against our wills. We must choose to sin and deliberately give him an opportunity to influence our lives. As Ron Susek has written, "Satan can only incite sinful behavior where he finds agreement in the human heart."[4]

James' remedy for the ungodly desires that ravage rebellious hearts and tear our churches apart is unapologetically forthright. Confession and repentance are necessary to restore our broken relationship with God and other believers. James writes,

> Submit yourselves, then, to God. Resist the devil, and he will flee from you. Come near to God and he will come near to you. Wash your hands, you sinners, and purify your hearts, you double-minded. Grieve, mourn and wail. Change your laughter to mourning and your joy to gloom. Humble yourselves before the Lord, and he will lift you up (James 4:7-10).

Crucial Questions

Psalm 51 records King David's response to God following his adulterous affair with Bathsheba. A repentant heart enabled him to see his sin from God's point of view and helped him examine the deeper areas of his life. David prayed, "Surely You [God] desire integrity in the inner self, and You teach me wisdom from deep within... God, create a clean heart for me and renew a steadfast spirit within me" (Psalm 51:6,10).

With James' teaching and King David's example in mind, take a few moments to ask yourself some very challenging but important questions as you consider an actual or potential conflict in your church.

- Have I wanted something so badly in this conflict that I'm willing to do anything to get it? (James 4:1-2)

- Is there any unconfessed sin in my life that has given Satan an opportunity to work in my heart and life? (Ephesians 4:27; 1 John 1:9)

- Am I obedient to God's Word? (1 John 5:3)

- Do my attitudes and actions at church show that I have a submissive heart? (Eph. 5:21; Philippians 2:3-4)

- Have I examined my own life before approaching others about their sin? (Matt. 7:3-5)

- Are my actions motivated by a deep commitment to "building up" the Body of Christ? (1 Thessalonians 5:11; 1 Corinthians 14:12; Jude 20)

The plain truth of the matter is that you might be the greatest problem in your church and not know it! Jesus noted this human tendency when he asked, "Why do you look at the speck of sawdust in your brother's eye and pay no attention to the plank in your own eye?" (Matthew 7:3)

Part of the Problem or Solution?

How can you know if you're part of the problem or part of the solution to a conflict in your church? Jesus taught that a person's outward actions or "fruit" provide a window into his or her heart (Luke 6:43-45; John 15:1-8; Matthew 7:16). Paul is even more direct:

> The acts of the sinful nature are obvious: sexual immorality, impurity and debauchery; idolatry and witchcraft; hatred, discord, jealousy, fits of rage, selfish ambition, dissensions, factions and

> envy; drunkenness, orgies, and the like. I warn
> you, as I did before, that those who live like this
> will not inherit the kingdom of God. But the
> fruit of the Spirit is love, joy, peace, patience,
> kindness, goodness, faithfulness, gentleness
> and self-control. (Galatians 5:19-23)

If your heart is filled with hatred, envy, or ambition,
you're part of the problem at your church. If you can't
control your temper or if you create any division among
church members, you're contributing to the conflict.
However, if you are bearing the fruit of the Spirit, then
God can use you to help resolve the conflict in your
congregation. As James wrote, "Peacemakers who sow in
peace raise a harvest of righteousness" (James 3:18).

Making peace is not easy, especially in the heat of
conflict. It is impossible to make peace without the power
and fruit of God's Spirit in your life. So resolve today to
"live by the Spirit, and you will not gratify the desires of
the sinful nature" (Galatians 5:16). Then your heart will be
at peace and Satan won't have an opportunity to use you
for his unholy purposes. You will be a peacemaker who
receives and gives God's blessings.

> Blessed are the peacemakers, for they will be
> called sons of God (Matthew 5:9).

Before you proceed with this book, take time to pray to
God about the spiritual condition of your heart. Relinquish
any wrong motives or sinful desires and commit to
bearing the fruit of righteousness in peacemaking.
Consider this prayer as your own.

> Father, I love and care about Your Church
> because I know that Your Son gave Himself on
> the cross to make her holy, clean, radiant, and

blameless. I know that it grieves Your heart when there is discord and disunity.

Cleanse my heart of any unrighteousness. Take away any wrong motives or desires, replacing them with godly attitudes. Allow me to see what You want my church to become, and my purpose in that vision. Give me a submissive heart – give me the strength to choose submission over my own will, opinion, and desire. Give me a hunger for the truth of Your Word over the truth of my experiences. Show me how to be a builder, a peacemaker, in my church and convict me through Your Holy Spirit when I am in error.

I ask for a heart of forgiveness. Give me the courage to go to those whom I have offended and ask for forgiveness and reconciliation, for the sake of Your name, for my witness, and for Your Church. In Jesus name, Amen.

The War Among Us

Pastor Joe, senior pastor of First Friendly Church, drove wearily to the local Christian bookstore to buy a couple of books on church conflict. "Maybe," he thought, "just maybe I can find some books to help me know what to do next. I'm at my wits' end."

As Joe walked up to the clerk and asked him if he had any books on the subject, the man wisecracked, "Oh, you want to read about the war zone!" Joe winced as the truth of the clerk's comment hit home.

Unfortunately there's more truth to the clerk's comment than most of us realize. One source estimates that more than 19,000 congregations experience major conflict every year.[5]   Only 2% of church conflict involves doctrinal issues; the other 98% is interpersonal in nature.[6] Too many churches have forgotten Jesus' words as he cleansed the temple, "My house will be called a house of prayer" (Matthew 21:13). Too many churches fight instead of pray, creating war zones strewn with spiritual casualties.

A survey of 506 pastors revealed that 95% of those questioned had experienced conflict at some point in their ministries, and 20% were embroiled in conflict at the time of the survey. Sadly, only 16% of the pastors reported reconciliation as a positive outcome of the conflict. Nearly four in ten pastors left their positions due to conflict, and a similar percent of church members (38%) eventually left their congregations.[7]

What do you think causes most of the conflicts in churches: Conflict with leadership, control issues/power struggles, spiritual immaturity, or prejudice? The survey cited above revealed that control issues were the most common cause of conflict (85%).

At First Friendly Church, Pastor Joe and the trustees approved switching the locations of the organ and piano in the sanctuary. When one church member learned of the change, she objected angrily, exclaiming, "Over my dead body!" She didn't have a good reason for objecting. She just wanted her way. She demanded control.

When we quench the Holy Spirit's presence in our lives we allow Satan to have an opportunity or foothold in our hearts. Once that happens, it is a matter of time until conflict erupts. When Christ is not the Lord of our lives and Head of our congregations, we assume control – and that's when war breaks out among us.

First Friendly Church had a treasurer who became increasingly controlling with church funds. On one occasion the treasurer made a motion at a church business meeting to spend a large amount of money for a renovation project. When the motion failed, he angrily resigned as treasurer and left the congregation. The next week he refused to turn over documents for several certificates of deposit, claiming that he had the right to keep them because he had given most of the money for them.

The treasurer was wrong and didn't have a legal basis for keeping the funds. His attitude and actions illustrate how easy it is to become possessive and controlling in the Body of Christ.

Christ Is Head of His Church

The Bible clearly teaches that God appointed Christ as "head over everything for the church" (Ephesians 1:22), an appointment that includes overseeing everything and everyone! Furthermore, we are called to conform to Christ's will by growing "up into him who is the Head, that is, Christ" (Ephesians 4:15).

> Christ is head of the church. He is the Savior of the body.
> *Ephesians 5:23, HCSB*

When the Apostle Paul described the false teachers who threatened the church at Colossae, he knew they didn't "hold on to the head [i.e., Christ], from whom the whole body, nourished and held together by its ligaments and tendons, develops with growth from God" (Colossians 2:19, HCSB).

Christ as Head of the Church has several profound and practical implications for our congregations. First, our very life comes from Christ (Colossians 3:3-4). When we lose our sense of connectedness to Christ, we'll suffer and become spiritually unhealthy. Second, our identity is found in Christ (Galatians 3:26-29). As Christians we literally bear His name; we are clothed in Him and belong to Him as co-heirs in God's family. Third, our unity is centered in Christ (John 17:20-23). This is a supernaturally imparted reality that is based on Christ's oneness with God the Father. Fourth, our purpose is determined by

Christ's Great Commission (Matthew 28:18-20). He calls us to make disciples of the nations.

When conflict envelops your church, remember Christ is the Head of your congregation – not you, church leaders, nor anyone else. Christ is not a figurehead or the honorary chairman of your congregation. He is the King of kings and Lord of lords (Revelation 19:16) who walks among the churches in righteous judgment (Revelation 1:9-3:22). Christ doesn't ask you to agree with Him; He deserves and expects your submission to Him (Luke 6:46) and to other believers (Ephesians 5:21).

It's Not Your Church!

Your church is not your church. It belongs to Christ, and you belong to Him!

Christ has not told us the color of carpet to buy for our church buildings, but He is clear about how we should conduct ourselves as we walk on that carpet. Christ has not told us whether our church budget should be higher or lower next year, but He demands that we give our all to follow Him. Christ has not told us whether to build a new facility or begin a new program, but He inspired the Apostle Paul to write these words to His Church throughout the ages:

> May the God who gives endurance and encouragement give you a spirit of unity among yourselves as you follow Christ Jesus, so that with one heart and mouth you may glorify the God and Father of our Lord Jesus Christ (Romans 15:5-6).

Devil Talk

Following the monthly fellowship dinner at First Friendly Church, Carol couldn't find the salad bowl she brought to the dinner. Standing near a group of people that included some first-time guests to the church, she exclaimed, "I can't believe someone would steal my bowl! This is supposed to be a church full of Christians!"

Later Carol found her bowl, stored in a place that was different than usual. She happily retrieved her bowl and went home oblivious to the damage she did to the reputation of the church. Carol will be back next Sunday. However, the guests who overheard her will not. Their "first-time impression" was not impressive.

Satan is the master of accusation. Revelation 12:10 describes him as "the accuser of our brothers...who accuses them before God day and night." Satan cannot destroy God's people, but he uses the powerful weapon of accusation to damage their integrity and diminish their influence. He strikes preemptively, knowing the destructive power of unsubstantiated accusation.

When Pastor Martin arrived at Pure Valley Church, church members described their anguish and heartbreak over what had happened to the previous pastor. A young woman in the congregation had accused the pastor of forcing her into sexual immorality and the church administrative council immediately placed him on paid leave. Charges were filed and local media headlined the story. There were no witnesses; it was her word against his word.

Two months later the council asked the pastor to resign, though he vigorously denied the charges and the case was still under investigation. He left town in disgrace. Later the charges against him were dropped due to a lack of evidence. Subsequent information surfaced indicating this was not the first time the woman had accused a minister of sexual impropriety.

Accusation is devastating. The pastor and his family suffered enormously, the church's ministry languished for several years, and the cause of Christ was ridiculed.

The Accuser

Accusation against the people of God is one of the primary ways Satan maintains his influence in the world and achieves his diabolical goals. He sought to discredit Job's faith and righteousness (Job 1:10-11), and he'll pursue every avenue possible to bring you and your church into disrepute.

Slander is a false report maliciously spoken with an intent to damage the reputation of a person or group. It shouldn't be surprising then, to discover that the word "Devil" literally means "slanderer." He slanders or falsely accuses by his very nature and incites others to follow his example. Regrettably, when Christians offer Satan a sinful foothold in their lives (Ephesians 4:27), they become his unwitting accomplices against their fellow believers. As Ron Susek has observed, "When satanic provocation finds heartfelt agreement [in a believer's mind], there is no limit to the destructive potential.... What the bodiless antagonist from hell cannot do alone, Satan achieves through those who welcome his voice."[8]

> The tongue also is a fire, a world of evil among the parts of the body. It corrupts the whole person, sets the whole course of his life on fire, and is itself set on fire by hell.
> James 3:6

Have there been times when you have entered into an unholy partnership with the slanderer, the Devil? It's easier to do than you might think. Your thoughtless, hasty accusations overheard by others can damage a believer's life and witness. Spreading gossip is the most common and tempting way to slander a brother or sister in Christ. If a fellow church member offends you and you complain to others without going to that person first (Matthew 18:15-17), Satan is using you to destroy a person for whom Christ died.

Slander, or any ungodly use of speech, has serious results in the lives of those who practice it. The Old Testament states that those who make false accusations face the following consequences:

- God will not acquit those who make false charges (Exodus 23:6-7)

- The false accuser receives God's punishment (Proverbs 19:5)

- The slanderer will perish (Proverbs 21:28)

The New Testament contains additional warnings for believers to avoid slanderous "devil talk" and its devastating consequences. Paul commanded believers in three churches to stop falsely accusing their fellow Christians: "Remind [the church at Crete]...to slander no one" (Titus 3:2); "But now you must rid yourselves of all such things as...slander..." (Colossians 3:8); "Get rid of all...slander" (Ephesians 4:31). Peter commanded believers living throughout Asia Minor to "rid yourselves of all...slander" (1 Peter 2:1).

Apparently slander was just as prevalent in New Testament churches as it is in congregations today. In 1 Peter 2:1, the Apostle Peter uses a strong word to command Christians to stop slandering one another. He tells us to "rid" ourselves once and for all of false accusation, doing it as intentionally and completely as taking off an undesirable soiled garment. It's heartbreaking to see how many professing Christians tolerate more slanderous filth in their speech than dirt on their clothes.

An Unwitting Accomplice?

Evaluate your life to determine if you've been an unwitting accomplice for Satan. Do you have a critical, accusatory spirit? Do you tolerate or spread gossip? A spirit of accusation permeates a church like a disease and can become a way of life within the congregation. Grumbling and complaining can turn into false accusation as we give credence to the dissatisfaction of other people. Gossip and godless chatter "will spread like gangrene" (2 Timothy 2:17) and quickly poison a church.

You influence the climate of your church by your speech. The Apostle Paul reminds us of the close connection between our daily conversation and the health of our relationships both outside and inside our congregations by writing, "Since you put away lying, speak the truth, each one to his neighbor, because we are members of one another...No rotten [unwholesome] talk should come from your mouth, but only what is good for the building up of someone" (Ephesians 4:25,29, HCSB).

> If you engage in any form of godless conversation, you must cleanse your heart first, then your speech.

Lead by example. Influence others through the power of godly speech. Put away lying and ungodly conversation, be truthful and speak only what will build others up. Your wholesome, godly and edifying speech will throw water on the raging fire of uncontrolled tongues and strengthen the Body of Christ.

Conflict from God's Perspective

Pastor Larry couldn't understand what was different at Changing Winds Church. He knew that the "honeymoon" stage of his pastorate wouldn't continue indefinitely; it only lasted a year. Since then something had changed in the congregation. People didn't seem to embrace Larry's leadership and vision for the future. Business meetings were becoming increasingly difficult. Unhappy church members were either sabotaging Larry's ministry ideas or leaving the church without an explanation.

Larry could sense the hand of the Enemy in all of this, but he didn't know what to do. Pastor Larry and Changing Winds Church were in the middle of a war and didn't realize it. Satan's "fingerprints" were everywhere, evident in the negative attitudes, harsh words, accusations, and increasing polarization of the congregation. Outreach to the community was almost nonexistent. The church was preoccupied with its problems.

Pastor Larry became absorbed with the issues and personalities that appeared to be the problems at Changing Winds Church, overlooking the deeper spiritual realities behind them. He lost sight of the fact that the Devil was on the prowl, actively seeking to devour him and his congregation (1 Peter 5:8). He forgot that his "struggle is not against flesh and blood, but against...the spiritual forces of evil" (Ephesians 6:11-12). Unfortunately, since Larry overlooked these realities, so did others in his congregation.

Do We Really Believe God's Word?

We must decide once and for all if we really believe what God's Word tells us about spiritual warfare. We either do or do not have an Adversary who is intent on destroying us. Satan either does or does not seek to incite sin in our lives so we participate in his schemes against the

Church. Accusation, lying, and hopelessness either have or do not have their ultimate source in the Devil.

Church Conflict from God's Viewpoint

The Apostle Paul clearly distinguishes between the spiritual and unspiritual way of viewing life in 1 Corinthians 2:12-13. He writes,

> We have not received the spirit of the world but the Spirit who is from God, that we may understand what God has freely given to us. This is what we speak, not in words taught us by human wisdom but in words taught by the Spirit, expressing spiritual truths in spiritual words.

If we believe what God has told us in His Word, His Spirit gives us the ability to perceive spiritual realities behind our experiences. Often our first response is from a human – and faulty – perception. Believers have so much more at their disposal. We have the wisdom of God, given freely, to help us understand the very real and present spiritual realm of our existence.

How does this truth help us with church conflict? First, we understand that our true enemy is Satan and not other people. No matter how hurtful or difficult others might be, Satan's power and influence are at the heart of their behaviors. Seeing them from God's perspective enables us to view them not as victimizers but as victims in need of God's sanctifying grace. Second, God is greater than our Adversary, Satan. By giving the outcome of the conflict over to God, we experience release from the turmoil that can so easily darken our hearts. God is greater than our church problems, and as we give ourselves to Him daily, He shows us how to be "peacemakers who sow in peace"

(James 3:18). Third, we know with confidence that Satan is defeated. He prevails over us only if we allow him to deceive us.

God will use you to promote peace in the midst of conflict if you see what is happening in your church through His eyes. This ability does not come naturally; it is supernaturally imparted through the revelation of God's Word and the empowering presence of His Spirit.

Answer the following questions to determine if you are ready to become an instrument of God's peace and experience "the working of His mighty strength" (Ephesians 1:19) in the most difficult of situations.

- Do you believe in the reality of Satan?

- Do you believe he is a defeated enemy of God?

- Do you believe God is in control of everything?

- Do you believe God's Spirit empowers you?

- Do you perceive life using spiritual wisdom?

- Do you believe you can be a peacemaker?

- Do you believe you can lead your church through conflict?

- Where are your circles of influence? Do you use them to bring biblical peace and unity to your church?

As the first chapter of this book ends, take a few moments to meditate on the Apostle Paul's prayer on the next page. Ask God to prepare you to be a leader in the days ahead by revealing Himself and His ways to you.

I keep asking that the God of our Lord Jesus
Christ, the glorious Father, may give you the
Spirit of wisdom and revelation, so that you
may know him better. I pray also that the eyes
of your heart may be enlightened in order that
you may know the hope to which he has called
you, the riches of his glorious inheritance in the
saints, and his incomparably great power for us
who believe (Ephesians 1:17-19a).

Spiritual battles must be fought using spiritual means.
Your effectiveness in helping to lead your congregation
through conflict will not depend solely on what you know
but on what you become and do as God makes you an
instrument of His peace.

When Two or Three Disagree

Conflict is inevitable, even among Christians. As an unbelieving world watches, it is imperative that those who follow Christ distinguish themselves in the ways they address conflict and promote peace. This chapter defines conflict and presents God's plan for resolving and preventing church conflict. His solution is clearly described in scripture: 1) understand the motives behind destructive and constructive conflict, 2) confront sin, 3) offer grace, 4) grow up and mature in Christ, and 5) preserve the precious gift of unity that God's Spirit gives us.

Motives Matter

The motives behind our actions matter to God. He cares little for our outward appearances but He cares intensely about the condition of our hearts. He searches our hearts – in places no one else can find – and He judges our actions according to what He finds there. God's Word admonishes those with impure motives and exalts the upright of heart. Our course may seem right to us, but God weighs our motives: "All a man's ways seem right to him, but the LORD weighs the heart" (Proverbs 21:2). Motives matter!

Behind every conflict lie human motives. To understand conflict we have to look at what motivates, or drives the conflict. The outcome of conflict is closely linked to the motives behind it. Since motives can be divided into two types – impure and pure – the conflict that arises from these motives is either destructive or constructive in nature.

We can find many examples of both types of conflict in the Bible. Destructive conflict involves the outward expression of sinful desires – impure motives – that break fellowship with God and other people. Constructive conflict occurs as God's people, with pure motives, address issues of biblical truth, doctrinal purity and church discipline. Thus, not all conflict is undesirable. But when conflict emanates from ungodly motivation, the destruction can be widespread. Only God's direct intervention or His use of godly people can turn the devastating tide.

Destructive Conflict

In chapter 1 we learned to be on guard against Satan's attempts to influence us to be unwitting accomplices in his attacks. If we don't guard our hearts, and our deepest motives, we contribute to his devastation. When selfish and sinful demands ignore the needs of others, both the unity and effectiveness of our congregations are destroyed. Remember, an ounce of prevention is worth a pound of cure! The remedy for a sinful heart condition calls for preventative medicine – the right diagnosis of motive, confession, repentance, and undivided obedience to God's Word.

Sometimes we can't see the offensive ways in our hearts. That's why we ask God to search our hearts, to penetrate to the deepest parts, expose our motives, make us pure, protect us from the enemy's temptations, and get rid of anything that would destroy the unity within the body of believers or our own witness.

> Search me, O God,
> and know my heart;
> test me and know my
> anxious thoughts.
> See if there is any
> offensive way in me,
> and lead me in the
> way everlasting.
> *Psalm 139:23-24*

Destructive conflict permeated many aspects of congregational life in the church at Corinth. Paul urged the

Corinthians to have no divisions among them, being "perfectly united in mind and thought" (1 Corinthians 1:10). He wanted their motives to be pure and their hearts to be united. Paul pleaded with two women in the church at Philippi "to agree with each other in the Lord" (Philippians 4:2). Presumably these two women were not in doctrinal error; their disagreement appears to be relational. They were serving Christ but were not reconciled with one another. One or both were nursing wrong attitudes, wrong motives. Their disagreement was affecting the spiritual life of the congregation. That's why Paul brought it to the church's attention.

An adult Bible study class wanted to help one of their ill members. Edith volunteered to plan and schedule meals to the member's home. Janice brought her meal to the church as scheduled, but discovered on arriving that plans had been changed and her meal wasn't needed. Irritated at the mistake, Janice confronted Edith. The confrontation escalated and soon the women wouldn't speak to one another. After several attempts at reconciliation, Janice eventually gave up and settled for an embittered relationship. Pride kept Edith from desiring restoration in their friendship.

How unfortunate! What started out as a positive ministry effort ended in a bitter, long-term conflict. A spirit of discord settles in when conflict is not resolved. Not only are relationships strained, the effectiveness of the church body is hindered.

> Destructive conflict involves the outward expression of sinful desires - impure motives - that break fellowship with God and other people.

Our book will examine many cases of destructive conflict. We'll see how God reveals the underlying motives that drive the conflict. This will help you identify the sources of conflict and find the best prescription for a cure!

Constructive Conflict

Destructive conflict is driven by ungodly motives and desires and is spread by contentious people. Constructive conflict is initiated by godly church leaders and members. While sometimes as unpleasant to experience as destructive conflict, constructive conflict may be necessary to preserve the integrity of the gospel and the purity and unity of Christ's Church. This kind of conflict is constructive because of its motivation, methods and outcomes.

An example of constructive conflict occurring frequently in the New Testament involved the apostles' confrontation of false teachers. In Acts 15:2 Paul and Barnabas entered into a "sharp dispute and debate" with false teachers who had infiltrated the church at Antioch. Paul warned Timothy about those who advocated "false doctrines" and who did not agree with the "sound instruction of our Lord Jesus Christ" (1 Timothy 6:3). In Galatians 2:4-5, the apostle denounced the "false brothers" who sought to bring Christians into legalistic bondage. Peter warned the readers of his second epistle about false teachers among them who "secretly introduce destructive heresies" (2 Peter 2:1-3). Confrontation when properly motivated is one way believers protect the body of Christ. Examine the following scriptures for further examples of constructive conflict: Romans 16:17-18, 1 Corinthians 5:1-5, 1 Timothy 1:3-6, 2 Timothy 3:1-5, and Titus 3:9-11.

> Constructive conflict occurs as godly people proactively confront issues or people that threaten the integrity of the gospel or the purity and unity of Christ's Church.

In each of these passages, God's people were motivated by love to instruct and correct the church. Congregational leaders were driven by a resolute commitment to the truth of the gospel as they sought to ensure the spiritual health of their churches.

Leaders are responsible to God to address error when it is discovered. As a matter of fact, all believers are called to address error in the Body of Christ. The following verses offer instruction for confrontation that ultimately serves to purify the Body of Christ:

> Brothers, if someone is caught in a sin, you who are spiritual should restore him gently. But watch yourself, or you also may be tempted (Galatians 6:1).

> If your brother sins against you, go and show him his fault, just between the two of you. If he listens to you, you have won your brother over (Matthew 18:15).

There are times when these instructions are followed with pure motives but don't result in restoration or reconciliation. Regardless of the outcome, we are accountable to obey them faithfully. God will use our obedience to deepen our relationship with Him and build up our congregations according to His timetable and purposes.

God's Strategy for Addressing Conflict

The God who created us knows our innermost thoughts and motives. He also knows how His children should resolve their difficulties. God's Word offers a divine guideline for confronting all of our problems and conflicts.

What is God's strategy for addressing church conflict? Confront it! – privately, gently, lovingly, prayerfully, and, if necessary, publicly. Too many Christians avoid conflict by ignoring it or simply moving to another congregation. Others resort to resolving conflict with their own wisdom and methods. All of these approaches make problems worse, not better.

Christ is looking for Christians who are passionately committed to preserving the integrity, purity, and unity of His bride, the Church. He's seeking believers who will take a leadership role in confronting destructive conflict using the Bible as their guide, and their commitment to the health of their congregations as their motivation.

Confront Sin

Pastor Daryl knew that he should address a growing problem in one of the Sunday School classes at Peaceful Rivers Church. The teacher was unhappy with several new ministries at the church. Rather than talk to the pastor or with the leaders of the ministries, the teacher expressed his discontent to class members, sometimes during the Sunday School lesson. Negativity and suspicion began to dominate the attitudes and conversations of class members. Pastor Daryl knew that he should do something about the situation, but he was avoiding confrontation for fear it would escalate the problem. He prayed that the teacher and class would have a change of heart. They didn't.

Most of us don't like confrontation. Sometimes we avoid it at all costs. Yet failure to confront sin God's way creates havoc and leads to destructive conflict. Inaction makes matters much worse and pulls churches into a quagmire of confusion.

The Apostle Paul warned the Corinthians about the dangerous consequences of tolerating immorality in their congregation (1 Corinthians 5:1-8). He compared the presence of sin to yeast, writing "don't you know that a little yeast permeates the whole batch of dough? Clean out the old yeast so that you may be a new batch"

(1 Corinthians 5:6b-7a). If we fail to address sin in our midst, we fail the person trapped by sin. Our goal is restoration – to help the person face his or her sin, confess it, and be restored to spiritual health.

Unconfessed sin in a Christian's life is like a malignant cancer in the human body. The victim is unaware of the disease until it begins to cause pain or damage. Likewise, sin is a cancer that destroys those who allow it to run its course. Unconfessed sin can cripple the believer's life and tear congregations apart. Sin always confuses, distorts and divides.

We shirk our responsibility to confront for identifiable but indefensible reasons. First, confronting others with their sin is unpleasant. It's the last thing most Christians and even church leaders want to do. Second, we might neglect confrontation because we misinterpret the admonition in Matthew 7:1-5, "Do not judge." We might believe that it is wrong for us to make judgments regarding sinful behavior in the life of another believer. Third, sometimes we avoid confrontation because we are fearful. We fear rejection, reprisal or litigation. Fourth, we refuse to confront because all too often we just don't care enough. We are responsible to one another and for one another in the Church of Jesus Christ. Because we are members of one another, we must speak truthfully to one another (Ephesians 4:25), even when it's not easy or pleasant.

Christ is more concerned with the purity and holiness of His bride, the Church, than with our level of comfort or discomfort. He desires for us to experience His powerful presence in our churches and for us to have a vibrant, positive testimony to the unbelieving world. This means that we might have to experience the discomfort of confronting an erring brother – or the even more painful prospect of accepting the corrective hand of a fellow believer upon our lives.

Spiritual Surgeons

God's Word shows us how to cut out the malignancy of sin that threatens the spiritual vitality of our churches. God's methods require the delicate skill of a trained surgeon. Without it we are engaging in spiritual malpractice. We must accurately follow God's surgical procedures.

Scrub up! We've already learned that we must check our motives when there is conflict. If we are confronting someone in sin, we must be doubly sure our motives and lives are clean!

We are called to help our fellow Christians remove the sin in their lives. Sometimes people quote Matthew 7:1 out of context to support passive, nonjudgmental tolerance: "Do not judge, or you too will be judged." However, Jesus does not prohibit his followers from making moral judgments in Matthew 7:1-5; rather, He commands them to examine their own lives first, applying God's standards to themselves before helping other believers deal with the sin in their lives.

> ...first take the plank out of your own eye, and then you will see clearly to remove the speck from your brother's eye (Matthew 7:5).

A Four-Step Process

In Matthew 18:15-17, Jesus outlined a four-step process for loving confrontation. The sinning believer's response determines whether or not the next step is taken, and each step involves a higher degree of accountability and corrective discipline. If he or she "listens to you" the process is happily finished. But if "he won't listen" or "pays no attention" the next step should be taken.

Step One: If Your Brother Sins

"If your brother sins against you, go and rebuke him in private. If he listens to you, you have won your brother" (Matthew 18:15). Some of the earliest Greek manuscripts for the New Testament omit the words "against you" from this verse, suggesting that a sin doesn't have to be a personal offense against us for us to address it. Galatians 6:1a supports this broader interpretation: "Brothers, if someone is caught in any wrongdoing…"

Jesus clearly tells us that we cannot ignore the presence of sin in our congregations once we're aware of its presence. He offers a radical approach to a life-threatening emergency. Like yeast that permeates a whole batch of dough (1 Corinthians 5:6), the sin of one believer ultimately affects everyone in the church. As the Apostle Paul writes in 1 Corinthians 12:26-27, "if one member suffers, all the members suffer with it…you are the body of Christ, and individual members of it."

Following God's plan for restoring a sinning brother is not easy. The thought of confronting someone in this manner may make you uncomfortable. You are not alone in these feelings. However, we cannot base our actions on feelings. "Rebuking" doesn't imply harshness. It means to make another believer aware of his or her sin in a convincing way. Sin is not rationalized or glossed over, but corrected lovingly and biblically.

Also, talk to the sinning believer privately, resisting the temptation to gossip with others about the sin. Gossip will not resolve the issue but make matters worse, most likely causing the sinning believer to be hurt and defensive rather than open and repentant.

Lois and Sarah served side by side on the women's planning committee and worked well together. Sarah was shocked when she learned that Lois had told another church lady that she disapproved of the work Sarah was doing. She immediately called Lois and inquired about her remarks. After denying several times that she had been gossiping about Sarah, Lois finally confessed and asked for forgiveness. Sarah willingly forgave and the issue was forgotten.

We can mistakenly believe that confrontation will escalate conflict. However, the principles for godly confrontation described in Matthew 18 are designed to bring restoration. God's plan works if we use it properly!

Step Two: Take One or Two Witnesses with You

Matthew 18:16 tells us what to do if our initial contact with the sinning Christian doesn't result in confession and repentance: "But if he won't listen, take one or two more with you, so that by the testimony of two or three witnesses every fact may be established" (HCSB). This approach underscores our love and concern for the sinning Christian and demonstrates that we will not give up on him or her.

Bringing "two or three witnesses" on the second visit follows the Old Testament procedure for establishing legal evidence (Numbers 35:30; Deuteronomy 17:6; 19:15), a process that was familiar to Christians during the first century and is helpful to us today. These witnesses should be loving brothers and sisters in Christ who are friends of the sinning believer and congregational leaders. Their presence underscores the need for repentance and restoration. They also can establish the facts of the situation in case the matter must be brought before the entire congregation.

> God's plan works if we use it properly!

Step Three: Tell the Church

"If he pays no attention to them, tell the church" (Matt.

18:17a, HCSB). There are several places in the New Testament that refer to congregational involvement in the spiritual discipline of a sinning Christian. By bringing the matter before the entire church, a new level of awareness and accountability is introduced, enabling the power of congregational prayer to be unleashed in the sinning Christian's life.

Remember, the goal of exposure is accountability that leads to full restoration. Exposure to humiliate or punish is not godly discipline. Love is the foundation and restoring the brother is the desired outcome.

Step Four: Treat Him Like an Unbeliever

"But if he doesn't pay attention even to the church, let him be like an unbeliever and a tax collector to you" (Matthew 18:17b, HCSB). Every opportunity is given to the errant believer to repent of his sin. If he repeatedly rejects overtures at all levels, the church must treat him "like an unbeliever" (i.e., Gentile) or "tax collector" (Matthew 18:17), causing him to experience consequences for his willful disobedience.

First-century Jews held Gentiles and Roman tax collectors in very low regard, avoiding them as much as possible. For Christians to treat an unrepentant member of the church in this way meant to cease having fellowship with him so that he would reconsider sinful actions, repent, and be restored to the fellowship of the church. The unrepentant believer's spiritual condition was not overlooked.

Biblical discipline is not punitive, but restorative (2 Corinthians 2:6-8). It is not hateful or vengeful, but loving and shows genuine concern for the spiritual welfare of those who are trapped by sin. Church discipline is an expression of God's love for his children "because the Lord disciplines those he loves" (Hebrews 12:6a).

Important Note

If your church leaders are considering church discipline, ask a Christian attorney to review your church bylaws and policies to ensure that the actions of your leaders will be consistent with your congregation's legal documents. Church discipline must be biblical in its approach, clearly described in your church bylaws and applied impartially.

Offer Grace

Let's face it. It's not easy to forgive someone who has wronged us. It seems unnatural to forgive – and it is! Genuine forgiveness is supernatural because it begins with God.

Getting What You Don't Deserve

Remember why and how God forgave you: "But God demonstrates his own love for us in this: While we were still sinners, Christ died for us" (Romans 5:8). God forgave you because He loved you, not because you did something to deserve His forgiveness. He loved you unconditionally even as you rejected Him and continued in your sinful ways. He loved you by taking the initiative to forgive you. As 2 Corinthians 5:21 says, "God made him [Jesus] who had no sin to be sin for us, so that in him we might become the righteousness of God."

You deserved judgment. God offered you grace. You deserved rejection. God offered you forgiveness.

Giving What Others Don't Deserve

Once we've made a personal decision to receive God's forgiveness through Jesus Christ, God calls us to live in a new way – His way! The Apostle Paul describes our new life in Christ by writing,

> Therefore, as God's chosen people, holy and dearly loved, clothe yourselves with compassion, kindness, humility, gentleness and patience. Bear with each other and forgive whatever grievances you may have against one another. Forgive as the Lord forgave you. And over all these virtues put on love, which binds them all together in perfect unity. Let the peace of Christ rule in your hearts, since as members of one body you were called to peace. And be thankful (Colossians 3:12-15).

True salvation changes our eternal destination and it changes our hearts. When we are saved we will live differently, including how we relate to one another in our congregations. To forgive as the Lord has forgiven you is more than a sentimental thought; it's a command! God expects us to extend to others what we have received from Him – grace and forgiveness.

The Meaning of Forgiveness

Forgiveness does not mean we overlook what others have done to us. Jesus expects us to lovingly confront those who have sinned against us (Matthew 18:15-17). Forgiveness is not forgetting. Try as you might, you can't forget what someone has done to you. Only God forgets when He forgives (Isaiah 43:25). Finally, forgiveness is not a feeling, although it does affect our feelings by removing bitterness from our hearts.

To forgive is to offer grace – undeserved favor – to those who have wronged us. It's a conscious, unilateral decision to reject the desire to make others pay for what they've done to us. Forgiveness changes our hearts. We desire to see God work in those who have wronged us, bringing His judgment, discipline, and grace into their lives. As Peter Barnes has written, "forgiveness is an act of faith. By forgiving another person, I am simply trusting that God is better at justice than I am, and I leave the issues of fairness to Him to work out. Wrong does not disappear when I forgive, but it does lose its grip on me, and God is able to redeem the brokenness of life."[9]

Kent and Marianne noticed the special bond between two deacons of the church they had been attending for three months. Obviously, the men were great friends. Watching their relationship was a major draw to the church. One day following services they described their observations to another church member. The church member laughed and said, "What you're seeing is a miracle! Three years ago those two decided to forgive each other for a feud that had lasted ten years. They hadn't spoken to each other in all that time. Yes, it's a miracle. Only Christ could bring those two together!" Kent and Marianne joined the church the next Sunday.

What if the guilty party remains unapologetic and unrepentant? Forgive as Christ has forgiven you. Unilaterally. Unconditionally. Lovingly. Don't be weighed down by an unforgiving heart and allow it to become a destructive barrier between you, God and others. As Abraham Lincoln once remarked, "The longer I carry a grudge, the heavier it gets."[10]

> Father...forgive us our sins, for we also forgive everyone who sins against us.
> *Luke 11:2-4a*

Bitterness will destroy your spiritual vitality like a cancer. Instead, offer grace to those who have wronged you, relinquishing the outcome to God and paying close attention to your attitudes and actions. And pray! Pray for truth, revelation, repentance, and restoration. Pray that your actions will glorify God and advance His kingdom through you and your church. God is still in the business of miracles and He can bring total healing to the most volatile of relationships if both parties surrender to His methods of reconciliation.

Reflect on the following questions and take as much time as necessary to deal with any issues of unforgiveness in your heart.

- Is there someone in your church who has wronged you?

- Have you prayed for God to examine your heart and to help you have Christ's forgiveness?

- Have you gone to the offending person to seek reconciliation?

- Did you receive an apology?

- Are you willing to forgive with or without an apology?

- Can you resist the temptation to get revenge?

- Do you trust God's justice and His timing in this situation?

- If the sin against you involves an illegal or immoral action, have you taken steps to protect others?

God doesn't ask you to forgive and forget. He commands you to forgive and wait expectantly for what He will do in you and in the person you've forgiven. When you offer grace to those who don't deserve it, you enable the Holy Spirit to work freely in your congregation. Walls of hurt, bitterness, and distrust are torn down. Healing begins, bringing new life and hope. As Rick Warren has observed, "Fellowship is a place of grace, where mistakes aren't rubbed in but rubbed out. Fellowship happens when mercy wins over justice... You can't have fellowship without forgiveness. God warns,' Never hold grudges' [Col. 3:13 LB], because bitterness and resentment always destroy fellowship."[11]

Grow Up in Christ

> *I won't grow up*
> *I will never even try...*
> *I'll never grow up, never grow up, never grow up*
> *Not me, not I.*
> *Never gonna be a man...*
> *Like to see somebody try*
> *And make me...*
> *I'll never grow up, never grow up, never grow up*
> *Not me, not me, not me, no sir, not me!*

Remember these catchy lyrics from the musical, *Peter Pan*? In a fantasy world, the thought of never having to grow up might be marvelous. Never growing up as a Christian is disastrous. When a person becomes a new Christian there is an expected and reasonable degree of immaturity. For the genuine believer, however new they may be, there is a hunger for more, a hunger for growth.

Sadly, there are too many people with Peter Pan dispositions in our churches today. Look at the song lyrics again. Do you detect a note of defiance? I won't grow up and no one can make me! When churches are filled with Peter Pan Christians – those who refuse to mature and grow up in Christ – you can be sure conflict is brewing. And guess who loves to keep you from maturing?

When Satan lost the battle for your soul and you became a Christian, he didn't give up trying to thwart God's purposes for your life. As noted in the first chapter of this book, Satan has an array of time-tested methods that he uses against you and your church. One tactic is to discourage you from growing spiritually and keep you, as the Apostle Paul would say, a "baby in Christ" (1 Corinthians 3:1, HCSB). Long-term spiritual immaturity prevents you from experiencing the blessings of deepening your relationship with Christ. It also creates a catalyst for conflict in your congregation. In fact, it's a given – where immature Christians gather, conflict will emerge.

Acts 18:1-18 describes how the Apostle Paul spent more than a year in Corinth, Greece, evangelizing and planting a new church in the city. The church was full of new Christians and Paul realized that they needed a basic spiritual diet before they progressed to the meat of God's Word. Paul addressed this issue when he described his visit by writing, "Brothers, I was not able to speak to you as spiritual people but as...babies in Christ. I fed you milk, not solid food, because you were not yet able to receive it" (1 Corinthians 3:1-2a, HCSB).

Paul taught new converts at their level of understanding, describing the elementary doctrines of the Christian faith as "spiritual milk." Paul knew that the Corinthians were not yet able to receive the "solid food" of the Christian faith. He had every expectation that their diet of spiritual food would change as their faith and service grew. You can imagine his disappointment when several years later he learned that they, in fact, were not growing. He pointed directly to their spiritual immaturity as the cause of the strife among them.

> ...you are still not able [to receive solid food] because you are still fleshly. For since there is envy and strife among you, are you not fleshly and living like ordinary people? (1 Corinthians 3:2b-3, HCSB).

What a mess! Why had the Corinthians succumbed to

Satan's schemes for their church? They were still spiritual babies! They refused to grow up! Consequently, they became susceptible to a wide variety of temptations and problems. Before long they allowed their fleshly desires to dominate their lives.

"Let's just leave! Let's all leave!" Ethel was just expressing everyone's feelings. The class of eight women was a tight-knit group. They stuck together. Now they were banning together in an all-out assault on the pastor. "He never listens to us and he knows how we feel. He's controlling and he's ruining our church. Things haven't been the same since he came here. When he removed the table we donated to the library that was the last straw. That shows how much he cares about us. Let's just leave! Let's all leave!"

Spiritual immaturity is rampant in churches today, resulting in unnecessary misery, difficulties and conflict. Churches are filled with immature Christians who lack biblical knowledge, Spirit-led discernment, and commitment to personal discipleship.

The central task of the Great Commission is to "make disciples" and to teach "them to observe everything I [Christ] have commanded you" (Matthew 28:19-20, HCSB). To teach and learn all that Christ has said requires intentional discipleship – much more than perfunctory glances at the Bible on Sunday mornings!

Intentional discipleship requires consistent in-depth study, meditation, and scripture memorization – and it requires life application of what is learned. The clear implication of the Great Commission is that we teach for obedience to Christ's command. We are to grow up in our salvation, move beyond our rebirth experience to a life of learning and growing. A disciple is spiritually alive and active, passionately desiring to know God deeply and follow Christ wholeheartedly. He or she delights in prayer, Bible study, fellowship, witnessing, giving, and ministry.

Are you a disciple of Jesus Christ? Has your relationship with God grown and matured over the years or are you still a spiritual infant, more focused on selfish pursuits than on becoming a fully devoted follower of Jesus Christ? The chart below delineates prevailing attitudes or beliefs of believers with childish faith contrasted to those with a mature faith. Which column best describes your way of viewing and living the Christian life?

Immature Believers	Mature Believers
I come to Sunday School (or worship). I don't need any other Bible study.	I can't get enough of God's Word. The more I study it, the more I need to study.
I'm saved and that's enough. Serving in ministry isn't going to get me any more saved.	I know I was saved to serve. How can I contribute?
I can worship by myself. Regular church attendance is legalistic.	I need other Christians. Together we are stronger than when we are alone.
What I say and do is my own business.	I'm accountable to my brothers and sisters in Christ.
I don't like to pray publicly.	May I pray for you?
My experience tells me…	God's Word says…
I'm not interested in serving at my church. I volunteer at the…	I know God gave me spiritual gifts to help build the church. I want to serve where God calls.
I can't afford to tithe. I can't pay my own bills now. God will just have to wait.	All I have belongs to God. I will give Him my first and my best.
My sin doesn't hurt anyone else. They live their lives, I live mine.	My witness is crucial. I'm called to live a holy life. God will empower me to obey Him.
I'm offended, so I'm not going to…	I forgive you.

I don't know enough to witness to someone about Christ.	I want to tell others what Christ has done for me.
I'm in charge of my life.	Christ is the Lord of my life. He is in control.

Preserve the Precious Gift of Unity

Slowly but surely, the ministries of Harmony Haven Church were grinding to a halt. People seemed to be more interested in arguing than in doing the Lord's work. Trust and fruitfulness in the kingdom of God were in short supply. Most church members could not remember when or how the problems began at Harmony Haven. A few members had vague memories of criticisms against one of the ministry directors. People took sides. Gossip and backbiting were prevalent. Yet no one quite remembered what the real issues were. They just knew they were a fractured, hurting congregation.

The Bible tells us exactly how we are to interact with others in the church. We are to avoid destructive conflict and build positive, Christ-centered relationships. As the psalmist noted, "How wonderful and pleasant it is when brothers live together in harmony!" (Psalm 133:1, NLT) But true unity accomplishes more than just fostering pleasant feelings among church members. God accomplishes His purposes through the unity of His people – "the hand of God was on the people to give them unity of mind to carry out what the king and his officials had ordered, following the word of the Lord (2 Chronicles 30:12). Not only is unity pleasant, it is essential for the work of God to flourish in a congregation.

What holds your congregation together when relationships become strained and tensions are high? What keeps your church focused on the purposes of God? Paul urged the Christians at Ephesus "to walk worthy of the calling you have received, with all humility and gentleness, with patience, accepting one another in love, diligently keeping the unity of the Spirit with the peace that binds us" (Ephesians 4:1-3, HCSB). There is a supernatural peace accessible to Christians and this peace will maintain unity. How do we acquire the peace that binds us together, especially in the midst of conflict?

Familiar Strangers

Rick Warren has observed that many churches are filled with "familiar strangers" – people who are acquainted with one another superficially. They are aware of certain facts about each other – such as names, number of children, and occupations – but they don't know each other's joys, struggles, and hopes.[12]

"Familiar strangers" often choose to worship together because they live in the same community, prefer the same church, like the same pastor, enjoy the same worship style, or appreciate the same ministry opportunities for their families. When everything at church is going according to their liking, all is well. But when it's not, watch out for problems!

Christ calls us to develop relationships based on commitment, not convenience or preference. He calls us to commit ourselves to His lordship and to one another, wholeheartedly and completely. He calls us to make commitments that are costly, requiring personal effort, time, and sacrifice.

A Precious Gift

The Bible teaches that when we receive Jesus Christ as Savior and become members of the family of God, we receive the precious gift of becoming one in Christ. We have "one Lord, one faith, one baptism, one God and Father" (Ephesians 4:5-6a) We are "baptized by one Spirit into one body," the Church of Jesus Christ (1 Corinthians

12:13). Through Christ we become more closely connected to one another than we are to our biological families!

Yet for this amazing spiritual truth to become a life-changing and church-transforming reality, we must be "diligent to preserve the unity of the Spirit in the bond of peace" (Ephesians 4:3, NASB). Our unity in Christ is a precious, fragile gift, not something that we created or deserved. Unity is a gift that comes with a tremendous responsibility – God's calling to zealously protect and cultivate it in our churches through the "bond of peace."

The Peace that Binds Us

When we accept God's love and forgiveness through Jesus Christ, our personal war with God ceases. Our wills stop striving against His will for our lives. A pervasive sense of well-being overshadows every aspect of our lives as we experience a new and exciting relationship with God through Jesus Christ.

This amazing experience with God overflows into our relationships with other people and especially other believers. Our peace with God becomes our peace with one another. We have a Spirit-empowered ability to relate to one another with humility, gentleness, and patience, "accepting one another in love" (Ephesians 4:2). This is the "peace that binds us" to one another, the peace that preserves our unity in Christ. This is the peace that keeps our congregations together when conflict threatens to tear them apart.

Peace in your church begins with peace in your heart. Have you experienced peace with God through Jesus Christ? A troubled relationship with God eventually spills over into

> Show family affection to one another with brotherly love. Outdo one another in showing honor.
> *Romans 12:10, HCSB*

our relationships with others.

God can use you to lead your church through the painful experience of conflict as you experience His peace in your daily relationship with Him. The peace of God radiating through you is the bond of peace that preserves unity in your church. Peace is the spiritual glue that holds you to your brothers and sisters in Christ.

Trouble at the Top

While newspapers decry corruption in the highest ranks of church leadership, this dilemma among God's people is not new. Our Adversary, the Devil, tries to topple the church by beginning at the top. Moses stood incredulous before Israel's most powerful spiritual leaders as they mounted an all-out preemptive strike against his anointed leadership. Even disagreements between church leaders, as with Paul and Barnabas, can create confusion. What should church members do? This chapter shows us how to address trouble at the top!

Seeds of Sedition

Pastor Mike of Sweet Fellowship Community Church was stunned to learn that his associate pastor, John, had accused him of misusing his authority. Those who knew about the accusation were upset and confused; the two men had appeared to have worked together very well for years. John was voicing a litany of complaints against his colleague, many of which were trivial or untrue, yet their impact on the congregation was staggering. Why would John do this?

Same Story, Different Place and People

Moses would understand Pastor Mike's surprise and dismay over the attack by his associate pastor. Moses had relied heavily on his two associates, Aaron and Miriam, as he led the Israelites through the rocky, barren Sinai wilderness. Aaron had stood beside Moses as they confronted the mighty Pharaoh of Egypt (Exodus 5:1) and later served as high priest in the tabernacle (Exodus 28).

Miriam was a gifted prophetess who led the women of Israel in praise and worship (Exodus 15:20-21).

Aaron and Miriam were more than Moses' trusted leadership team, they were his brother and sister! Yet family ties didn't quell the unrest and envy that eventually filled their hearts. Miriam and Aaron were unwilling to accept their God-given roles as they served under Moses' leadership. Perhaps they felt threatened by Moses' appointment of seventy elders to help govern Israel (Numbers 11:16-17). It's more likely that they wanted to share Moses' role and status in the spiritual life of Israel. What Aaron and Miriam did foreshadowed what happened at Sweet Fellowship Community Church and in many congregations today.

The Issue Was Not the Issue

"Miriam and Aaron criticized Moses because of the Cushite woman he married... They said, 'Does the LORD speak only through Moses? Does He not also speak through us?'" (Numbers 12:1-2, HCSB) What did Moses' marriage have to do with Miriam's and Aaron's desire to share Moses' prophetic role? Absolutely nothing! The issue of Moses' marriage was merely a pretext for their real agenda. Miriam and Aaron envied Moses' role as God's prophetic spokesman, and to elevate themselves they questioned the uniqueness of Moses' calling.

> For where envy and selfish ambition exist, there is disorder and every kind of evil.
> *James 3:16, HCSB*

Take a few moments to evaluate your attitude toward your spiritual leaders. It's tempting to become an "armchair critic" and question their leadership without first examining your own heart and motives. In the case of Miriam and Aaron, they questioned Moses' unique calling to be God's voice to Israel. They believed that God had spoken through them and used them for His purposes, which was true. However, this didn't mean that they were called to share Moses' leadership position. Aaron and Miriam overlooked an extremely important fact: God had called Moses – and not them – to serve as the leader of Israel.

Submission Isn't a Bad Word

At Sweet Fellowship Community Church, the associate pastor allowed an envious spirit to grow within him as he listened to the pastor's sermons. John began evaluating Pastor Mike's sermons with a critical spirit, believing that he could preach better than Mike. Perhaps he could. But John wasn't called to be the preaching pastor of Sweet Fellowship Community Church; God had called Mike to this ministry.

Rather than becoming envious and critical, John should have prayed for God's leading in his life. Instead of having a rebellious heart which increasingly rejected Mike's leadership, John should have expressed his feelings to Mike so that they could be discussed openly and prayerfully. Perhaps God was beginning to call John to a new kind of ministry. In the meantime, God expected John to have a submissive, trusting, and Spirit-controlled heart.

> Obey your leaders and submit to their authority. They keep watch over you as men who must give an account. Obey them so that their work will be a joy, not a burden, for that would be of no advantage to you.
> *Hebrews 13:17*

Christ has placed spiritual leaders in positions of authority because they have submitted themselves to His lordship. They know that they must give an account for the care of their congregations (Hebrews 13:17). They eagerly serve Christ's Church because they know that "when the Chief

Shepherd appears, [they] will receive the crown of glory that will never fade away" (1 Peter 5:4). As Lord of His Church, Christ is very capable of dealing with leaders whose attitudes and actions do not build up and strengthen a congregation. Christ cares deeply for the well-being and witness of His Body, the Church.

Take a few moments to answer the following questions in light of Hebrews 13:17

- What is the primary role of church leaders?

- What action and attitude should you have toward your leaders?

- Who benefits when you have the correct response to leaders?

Seeds of Sedition

Numbers 12:4-15 tells us how God dealt quickly and decisively with Miriam and Aaron. He judged their rebellious hearts and gave Miriam a severe case of leprosy to bring her and Aaron to a point of repentance and submission. Ironically, Aaron, the high priest who claimed to have the same relationship with God that Moses had, begged Moses to pray for Miriam's healing. Moses cried out to God and Miriam was restored. However, God banished Miriam from the camp of Israel for seven days, halting Israel's journey to the Promised Land and bringing public shame on her.

Miriam's punishment served as a sobering lesson for the Israelites. Still her rebellion planted destructive seeds of sedition among the people. As we'll see in the following pages of this chapter, Aaron and Miriam's

> The anger of the LORD burned against them.
> *Numbers 12:9a*

rebellion in Numbers 12 set a precedent for the widespread insurrections recorded in Numbers 14 and 16. People follow the example of their leaders!

The Fruit of Rebellion

The controversy grew at Sweet Fellowship Community Church as gossip among church members spread and distorted the associate pastor's allegations. Shock was replaced by suspicion. Could Pastor Mike really be misusing his authority? Were John's allegations true? The line between accusation and reality blurred as emotions ran high and battle lines formed. Church members who had enjoyed positive relationships with Pastor Mike began to believe John's allegations, even though their personal experience with Mike didn't support John's claims. Regrettably, it didn't take long for the seeds of sedition to develop and bear their terrible fruit – the fruit of rebellion.

Have you watched a group of children play the game, "Follow the Leader?" First, they select a leader and form a line. Next, each child intently scrutinizes the leader as the group walks in formation, seeking to mimic the leader's actions. The results can be quite comical! However, "Follow the Leader" at church is not child's play. When a leader strays the results are anything but comical.

At Sweet Fellowship Community Church, it didn't take long for other rebellious leaders to emerge as they rallied around the associate pastor. They didn't immerse themselves in prayer or take time to visit personally with the pastor to determine the truth of the situation. In their minds, the associate pastor's allegations were established facts. John's rebellious heart had influenced some of the leaders in the church, who in turn swayed others in the congregation.

Numbers 13-14 records a similar incident in the life of God's people. The Israelites had witnessed numerous miracles as God freed them from slavery in Egypt. Now they were about to take possession of the land God had promised them. Twelve spies were sent to survey the territory, men who were more than courageous adventurers or soldiers. They were leaders from the twelve tribes of Israel, chosen because of their position and influence among the people. The people trusted them.

After exploring the land for forty days, ten of the twelve spies gave a fearful, negative report. The spies had expanded the scope of the area they were sent to explore (to include the heavily populated areas near the Mediterranean Sea and Jordan River) and distorted what they had discovered (claiming that the land was filled with giants). They complained, "We can't attack those people; they are stronger than we are" (Numbers 13:31). By instilling fear into the people, they gained a loyal following in their rebellion. To gain support for their insurrection, the spies filled the assembly with discouragement by spreading the bad report among all the Israelites. With the disparaging report, they added lies and gross assumption: "The land...devours those living in it" [a lie] and "We seemed like grasshopper in our own eyes, and we looked the same to them" [an assumption] (Numbers 13:32-33).

We Can't!

Shammua. Gaddiel. Ammiel. These spies were well-known and respected in their day, but their names have faded into obscurity because they abdicated their responsibility to carry out God's plan for His people. They and seven other naysayers stated emphatically, "We can't" when presented with the challenge to live by faith and claim the promises of God. Their declaration was not about their ability. God had already promised them victory. Their mouths were shouting, "We can't" but their hearts were roaring, "We WON'T!" These shrewd leaders knew they could gain a following in their rebelliousness if they intimidated the people with the obstacles facing them. In their faithless rebellion they made the people believe their God was not able to do what He had promised. Biblical commentator Roy Gane offers this insight on the spies' rebellion: "For the person of faith, obstacles are temporary because God is real. For the disbeliever, obstacles are permanent because God is not real enough."[13]

What emboldened the ten spies to come directly against God's will for His people and Moses' leadership? How could they muster the audacity to disobey God? A strong possibility is the example set by Miriam and Aaron in Numbers 12. It's very likely their revolt had become widely known among the Israelites, making it easier for the ten spies to follow their example and rebel against God and Moses.

The ten spies also incited widespread grumbling and insurrection among the entire assembly. The unhappy Israelites were ripe for bearing the fruit of rebellion, and they readily followed the rebellious example of their new leaders.

We Must!

After hearing the report of the ten spies, the Israelites' euphoria over being near the Promised Land quickly vaporized into a panic-stricken uproar. Caleb, one of the twelve spies, offered a very different assessment. He silenced the people and declared, "We must go up and take possession of the land because we can certainly conquer it!" (Numbers 13:30, HCSB)

Caleb believed the promises of God. He believed what God told

> For God did not give us a spirit of timidity, but a spirit of power, of love and of self-discipline.
> *2 Timothy 1:7*

Moses at the burning bush: "I have come down to rescue [the Israelites] from the power of the Egyptians and to bring them from that land to a good and spacious land, a land flowing with milk and honey" (Exodus 3:8, HCSB).

With Joshua at his side, Caleb courageously confronted the other ten spies. He had seen the challenges of conquering the Promised Land, but he viewed them through the lens of faith. How could Caleb declare, "We must" when nearly everyone else said, "We can't?" Caleb's boldness rose out of his understanding of God, not the military capabilities of the Israelites. As Roy Gane has observed, "Faith is courage that conquers. Disbelief is cowardice that correctly assesses the impossibility of a situation but fails to take God into account."[14] Caleb wasn't about to leave God out of the equation.

God recognized Caleb's faith by saying, "my servant Caleb has a different spirit and follows me wholeheartedly" (Numbers 14:24). Caleb's spirit was noticeably different than the spirit of the ten rebellious spies. He had a wholehearted commitment to follow God anywhere, anytime, regardless of the challenges. Because Caleb abandoned himself completely to God, he was a leader worth following.

Follow the Right Leader

The Israelites had a choice. They could believe the faithless report of the majority (the ten spies) and follow them, or they could heed the minority report and follow Caleb. When there's trouble at the top – conflict between the leaders of God's people – be careful to follow the right leader for the right reasons. The membership of Sweet Fellowship Community Church didn't divide evenly between following Pastor Mike or siding with John. Yet enough members aligned with John to create division within the congregation. Much turmoil could have been avoided if church members had taken the time to carefully consider the fruit of their leaders' lives and actions.

Hebrews 13:7 instructs us to "remember your leaders who have spoken God's word to you. As you carefully observe the outcome of their lives, imitate their faith" (HCSB). Godly leaders possess a lifestyle and relationship with God that motivates others to have a similar faith.

One way to discern which leader to follow in a church controversy is to remember Caleb's example. A leader worth following displays the following four qualities.

A Passion for God

Caleb followed God wholeheartedly. He displayed confidence that the Israelites could "certainly do it" because he passionately believed God was in control and able to accomplish what He had promised to the Israelites. Caleb's desire to please God, not the whims of the people, held him on a steadfast course of obedience.

- God's leader shows unwavering devotion to God and what God is able to do in any situation

- God's leader consistently and earnestly seeks God's will before acting

- God's leader is more concerned about obeying God than what people say

Absolute Confidence in God's Word

Caleb believed God's promises concerning the Promised Land. He wasn't swayed by what anyone else believed or did. His charge to the people was in total concert with what God had already decreed. The spies had to resort to distortion and manipulation to win the people.

Caleb stuck to the truth.

- God's leader had nothing to hide, but operates in the open, offering full disclosure of factual information that helps resolve the situation

- God's leader acts in complete obedience to the whole counsel of God's Word

- God's leader focuses on biblical principles, not personal agenda, when seeking resolution

A Heart Submitted to the Leadership of Other Godly Leaders

Caleb submitted himself to Moses' leadership. He used his influence to support God's appointed leader and didn't seek his own following. If the people accepted Caleb's challenge, they would have followed God's anointed leader. The rebellious spies tried to usurp Moses' leadership as they contended for the people's loyalties.

- God's leader willingly submits to others in authority over him (welcomes accountability)

- God's leader supports and never undermines the leadership of others

- God's leader never seeks to divide people's loyalties to gain personal support

A Lifestyle of Fruitful Obedience

Caleb's obedience achieved the purposes of God for Israel. His words and actions glorified God, not himself.

- God's leader always points the people toward allegiance to God

- God's leader always points the people to accomplish the God-given purposes of the church

- God's leader seeks to glorify God and not exalt self in any manner

Pause now to thank God for your spiritual leaders and submit your heart to their leadership. They need your support and we are commanded in scripture to offer it. Determine today to stand in the gap for your leaders through prayer and supportive actions. Make it a joy for them to serve you.

Preemptive Strike

Military strategists know the power of first strikes. Catching the enemy's army unaware or, better yet, unprepared, usually ensures victory on the battlefield. When the enemy force is caught off guard, often it's too late to mount a successful counterattack.

At Sweet Fellowship Community Church, Pastor Mike reeled from the preemptive strike launched by his associate pastor. John had carefully developed the plan for voicing his accusations, deliberately choosing the time and place for his attack. This caught Pastor Mike completely by surprise. Not knowing what to do next, he fell to his knees in prayer, seeking God's guidance and intervention. Prayer was Mike's first response – not a last resort.

Blind Ambition

Serving as a spiritual leader is never easy, especially during times of controversy and conflict. Moses discovered this truth as he led the Israelites through some of their most difficult experiences in the wilderness.

One such time is described in Numbers 16. A Levite

named Korah, along with two other men, Dathan and Abiram, "became insolent and rose up against Moses" (Numbers 16:1-2). Before launching a preemptive strike against Moses' leadership, they recruited a formidable grievance committee to assist them – "250 prominent Israelite men who were leaders of the community and representatives in the assembly" (Numbers 16:2, HCSB). Korah and his allies had impressive credentials, forceful personalities, and powerful support. However, they lacked what Moses had – a vital, spiritual connection to the living God. Without God's blessing, their first strike was doomed to failure.

Korah's ambition took him down an incredibly presumptuous and dangerous path. He attacked Moses' and Aaron's leadership by saying, "You have gone too far! Everyone in the entire community is holy, and the LORD is among them. Why then do you exalt yourselves above the LORD's assembly?" (Numbers 16:3, HCSB)

Remember Korah's position among the Israelites. As a Levite Korah was responsible for caring for "the most holy objects" in the tabernacle (Numbers 4:4), assisting Aaron and the priests with worship. While Korah's role was important, it was secondary to Aaron's priestly functions and certainly not comparable to Moses' role as Israel's spiritual and political leader. Korah's insolent heart became discontent, eventually manifesting itself in blatant, shameless insurrection.

Korah's attack against Moses and Aaron employed a clever strategy that appealed to those who were looking for an excuse to rebel against authority. Korah voiced two general truths to arrive at a false (and illogical) conclusion/accusation. He correctly asserted that (1) everyone in Israel had been set apart and chosen by God, and (2) God was among the Israelites. However, these truths didn't negate the fact that God had given different roles and responsibilities to the Israelites. Contrary to

Korah's allegation, Moses and Aaron weren't exalting themselves as they served as leader and high priest of Israel. They were obeying God's calling for their lives. In reality, Korah was the one who sought to exalt himself above others.

Clearly, Satan doesn't need to rely on logic to achieve his diabolical schemes. Personal ambition and unchecked emotion will cause people to believe and do almost anything. They will misuse God's Word and spiritualize false accusations. Ironically, people with ungodly motives frequently will accuse spiritual leaders of doing what in fact they are doing. When a church is embroiled in conflict, it's amazing how easily Satan can blind people from recognizing these destructive tactics.

Take a few moments to consider carefully which of the following statements are appropriate applications of this account (Numbers 16) to churches today.

- Church leaders should always abide by the wishes of the majority of church members

- If a group of church members say they are acting directly from God, leaders should assume God has spoken on the matter

- Bringing ungodly accusation against God's appointed leader will end in judgment for the accuser (in some instances, even disaster)

- If a staff member tries to usurp the pastor's position and authority, he/she is wrong

- If enough people oppose a church leader, it usually indicates the leader is in the wrong

In response to Korah's rebellious acts, Moses proposed a test that must have made Korah and his followers smile with smug satisfaction. If God endorsed their actions and leadership, Moses said that they would continue to live life normally and eventually die natural deaths. However, if God approved Moses' and Aaron's leadership, He would do something unheard of and open the earth to swallow alive the rebels and their families. This, of course, was highly unlikely unless God intervened in the situation dramatically and supernaturally.

Numbers 16:31-32 describes what happened next: "As soon as he [Moses] finished saying all this, the ground under them split apart and the earth opened its mouth and swallowed them, with their households and all Korah's men and all their possessions." Dathan and Abiram met similar fates. When God's will was spurned, He acted decisively!

Don't Play with Fire!

The 250 members of Korah's grievance committee also met a dramatic end. They had aspired to the priesthood, disregarding the fact that only Aaron's family and descendents could serve as priests in Israel. Knowing what had happened to Aaron's sons when they offered incense with unauthorized fire, Moses proposed a test to reveal God's choice for the priesthood. He instructed the 250 to appear before God

> Aaron's sons Nadab and Abihu took their censers, put fire in them and added incense; and they offered unauthorized fire before the LORD, contrary to his command. So fire came out from the presence of the LORD and consumed them, and they died before the LORD.
>
> *Leviticus 10:1-2*

with bronze censers filled with incense and fire (priestly equipment used for worship). If the men had remembered

God's Word, they wouldn't have done this or even come close to the Tabernacle. God had clearly instructed Moses and the Israelites, "You are to appoint Aaron and his sons to carry out their priestly duties, but any unauthorized person who comes near [the sanctuary] must be put to death" (Numbers 3:10, HCSB).

Sure enough, God punished the insolence of the 250 by sending fire from heaven and incinerating them (Numbers 16:35). The 250 "wannabe priests flunked their test and received an F – 'F' for fire!"[15]

Bible commentator J. Magonet aptly summarizes the results of Korah's rebellion by writing, "ironically, while those who sought earthly power [Korah, Dathan, and Abiram] go down living into the earth, those who sought spiritual power [the 250], go up as a burnt offering to God."[16]

A variety of motives could have been behind John's actions against Pastor Mike at Sweet Fellowship Community Church, including jealousy, anger, insecurity, resentment, and selfishness. Nothing noble or pure was behind John's actions, regardless of the ways he rationalized them. Simply stated, he took matters into his own hands when he launched a preemptive strike against Pastor Mike, overlooking the Bible's clear instruction for conflict resolution in Matthew 18:15-17 and disregarding Mike's spiritual authority as the pastor of the congregation. The Bible clearly offers a better way for John to have expressed his feelings and concerns.

Responding to First Strikes

Moses' response to Korah serves as an excellent example for spiritual leaders today when they are attacked by members of their leadership teams or congregations:

- Moses fell "facedown" (Numbers 16:4) immediately after Korah's accusation. This was not an emotional reaction or fearful act of surrender but a spontaneous expression of humility and dependence on God. Moses responded similarly on other occasions when confronted by the rebellious people of Israel (Numbers 14:5,22; 20:6). His response was a genuine demonstration of his submission to God, an act which immediately falsified Korah's allegation: "Why then do you exalt yourselves...?" (Numbers 16:3)

- Moses prayed for God to act with justice and fairness (Numbers 16:22). He also felt free to express his emotion (anger) to God (Numbers 16:15).

- Moses waited on God to act, depending completely on God's intervention to resolve the situation. He resisted the temptation to take matters into his own hands.

- Moses did not defer leadership to the masses or to the rebellious leaders. He retained the leadership position and role God had given to him.

Leadership or Abuse?

There are clear distinctions between biblical leadership and spiritual abuse. This section carefully delineates them as we continue to consider church conflict involving "trouble at the top."

The worship leader at Song of Life Church believed that no one, including his senior pastor, should supervise his ministry at the church. Derek told Pastor Andy and others in the church that he was accountable "only to God" as he led the congregation in worship.

Predictably, it wasn't long until difficulties arose between Derek and Andy. One day Derek lashed out at his pastor, claiming that the pastor's efforts to approve the music for the worship services and oversee Derek's daily activities were "spiritually abusive." Was Derek correct or confused about his role as a staff member at Song of Life Church?

Biblical Leadership vs. Spiritual Abuse

The New Testament church selected leaders who were called and qualified to serve. For example, an overseer or elder had to be "above reproach, the husband of but one wife, temperate, self-controlled, respectable, hospitable, able to teach, not given to drunkenness, not violent but gentle, not quarrelsome, not a lover of money. He must manage his own family well...not be a recent convert... [and] have a good reputation" (1 Timothy 3:2-7).[17]   Deacons   were required to have similar qualifications (1 Timothy 3:8-13).[18] Leaders were not chosen quickly or carelessly; the fruit of their lives had passed the test of time before they were given positions of authority and responsibility.

> Therefore, as a fellow elder... I exhort the elders among you: shepherd God's flock among you, not overseeing out of compulsion but freely, according to God's will...
> *1 Peter 5:1-2, HCSB*

While the Bible does not mention the wide array of ministry titles and positions present in churches today, it does identify several general ministry roles in local congregations. Apostles or their representatives had the authority to "appoint elders in every town" to "direct the affairs of the church" (Titus 1:5; 1 Timothy 5:17). The office of elder was clearly distinguished from the office of deacon (Philippians 1:1; 1 Timothy 3:1-13). While elders exercised congregational oversight as one aspect of their ministries, deacons focused on service-oriented ministries.

There is a biblical basis for establishing roles, responsibilities, and lines of accountability in local congregations. Furthermore, spiritual leaders have overseeing/directing roles in the congregation. For example, the Apostle Paul appointed Timothy to be his personal representative to the church at Ephesus and instructed him to "preach the Word; be prepared in season and out of season; correct, rebuke and encourage – with great patience and careful instruction" (2 Timothy 4:2). Paul exhorted Titus to fulfill a similar role in the church at Crete, charging him with the task of "rebuk[ing] them sharply, that they may be sound in the faith" (Titus 1:13, HCSB).

Clearly, the senior pastor at Song of Life Church possessed the biblical authority to direct the activities of the music minister. This included, if necessary, the authority to rebuke, correct, and instruct the music minister. Exercising biblical leadership in these ways is not abusive or controlling. If done in the right manner and with godly motives, it can strengthen and encourage both the staff member and congregation.

There are clear distinctions between biblical leadership and spiritual abuse. Abuse involves the use of guilt, fear, intimidation, and control for self-serving purposes. Abuse disregards the needs and welfare of others. Most importantly, abuse involves sinful attitudes and practices that violate God's Word.

In their book, *The Subtle Power of Spiritual Abuse: Recognizing and Escaping Spiritual Manipulation and False Spiritual Authority within the Church*, David Johnson and Jeff VanVonderen define spiritual abuse by writing, "when your words and actions tear down another, or attack or weaken a person's standing as a Christian – to gratify you,

your position or your beliefs while at the same time
weakening or harming another – that is spiritual abuse."[19]

Johnson and VanVonderen add the following
clarifications to their definition of spiritual abuse:

- It is not abusive when a spiritual leader, who has the
  responsibility to make final decisions, uses his/her
  best judgment and chooses to go against your
  opinion...

- It is not abusive when a Christian (whether or not
  they are a leader) confronts another Christian
  because of sin, wrongdoing or even honest mistakes
  that must be corrected...

- Likewise, it is not abusive when a person in ministry
  or leadership is asked to step down from their
  position because of emotional, physical, mental or
  spiritual problems...

- It is not spiritually abusive or inappropriate to
  disagree, whether on doctrines or other issues, even
  in public...

- It is not abusive to hold to certain standards of group
  conduct...[20]

When Spiritual Leaders Are Abusive

Physical and sexual abuse must be dealt with
immediately and decisively, using the Bible and secular
laws to determine what steps should be taken. Church
leaders are not above the laws of the land, since "everyone
must submit to the governing authorities" (Romans 13:1,
HCSB, emphasis added). This teaching applies to everyone
in the church, including spiritual leaders.

Spiritual abuse generally is not addressed by the legal system. As Jesus noted, some of the worst abusers are not on the "lunatic fringe" of society but are widely accepted by secular authorities and the general population. Jesus denounced the motives and methods of the scribes and Pharisees, saying "don't do what they do, because they don't practice what they teach. They tie up heavy loads that are hard to carry and put them on people's shoulders, but they themselves aren't willing to lift a finger to move them.... Woe to you, scribes and Pharisees, [you] hypocrites...blind guides... snakes... brood of vipers!" (Matthew 23:1-33, HCSB)

Some forms of spiritual abuse are more obvious than others, since they bring immediate anguish and suffering to their victims (legalism, authoritarianism, and intimidation). Other kinds of abuse are more subtle, such as the kind of suffering that comes from living in the spiritual darkness of false teaching. Spiritual falsehood is dangerous and abusive since it limits a person's spiritual development and can even jeopardize his or her eternal destiny.

In chapter 4 of this book, we will see how the New Testament teaches congregations to take strong measures to remove false teachers from their midst. There must be no compromise in this area since false teaching undermines the very fabric and integrity of a congregation. Jesus didn't tolerate the falsehood and hypocrisy of the Pharisees. The Apostle Paul also used strong words to condemn false teachers:

> For such men are false apostles, deceitful workmen, masquerading as apostles of Christ. And no wonder, for Satan himself masquerades as an angel of light. It is not surprising, then, if his servants masquerade as servants of

righteousness. Their end will be what their actions deserve (2 Corinthians 11:13-15).

False teaching must be addressed promptly and decisively. But how does God expect us to respond to other forms of spiritual abuse that are not doctrinal in nature or don't involve physical or sexual abuse? How should we respond to ungodly treatment by people in positions of church leadership?

Trusting God to Resolve Spiritual Abuse

In his book *Under Cover*, John Bevere draws an important distinction between submission and obedience by writing, "Obedience deals with our responsive actions toward authority. Submission deals with our attitude toward authority. This is where most of us miss it."[21]   As Christians, we are called to have an unconditional attitude of submission toward all forms of God's delegated authority – in our homes, churches, workplaces, and government. We willingly choose to submit to these authorities because we have first submitted ourselves to God's direct authority and presence in our lives.

The Bible offers several key principles for understanding the relationship between authority, submission, and obedience.

- God has established all authority, which from our perspective might be just or unjust (Romans 13:1-3; 1 Peter 2:18).

- God will sometimes use unjust and unworthy authorities for His purposes (i.e., Pharaoh – Exodus 9:16; the Assyrian and Babylonian armies – Habakkuk 1:1-11). Eventually God will judge unworthy leaders and bring an end to their rule (see the examples of Saul in 1 Samuel 26:10 and 31:1-13, as well as Herod Agrippa in Acts 12). In the meantime, God calls us to trust Him and watch Him accomplish His purposes in our circumstances.

- We do not submit to God's delegated authorities because we happen to like or agree with those whom God has placed over us. As John Bevere has observed, "Submission does not mean, 'I submit as long as I agree.' Submission does not even begin until there's disagreement."[22] We submit to authority as an act of faith – from the heart. We bring judgment on ourselves and disrepute to the cause of Christ when we fail to have a submissive attitude toward authority (Romans 13:2).

- We must obey those in authority unless they demand that we do something that directly contradicts God's Word (Acts 5:29). Yet our disobedience doesn't give us the right to avoid the consequences of our actions or be disrespectful toward those whom God has placed in authority over us (i.e., David and Saul – 1 Samuel 24:1-7; 26:1-11; Shadrach, Meshach, Abednego and King Nebuchadnezzar – Daniel 3; Daniel and King Darius – Daniel 6; Peter and John before the Sandhedrin – Acts 4:18,19,31; Paul before the high priest Ananias – Acts 23:1-5). For believers, conditional obedience always takes place within the context of unconditional submission.

These principles apply to everyone in a church and especially when there's "trouble at the top" in a congregation. When the worship leader at Song of Life Church claimed that the senior pastor was abusing him spiritually, his attitude and actions clearly revealed an unsubmissive heart. He refused personal accountability and ignored biblical teaching regarding the relationship between authority, submission and obedience.

If the senior pastor had been guilty of spiritual abuse, the music minister should have approached him as a brother in Christ, lovingly and prayerfully, and followed the scriptural guidelines found in Matthew 18:15-17. God can break through interpersonal barriers and abusive behaviors when one or both parties understand the power of biblical submission.

Parting Company

Pastor Lindsey was called to be the senior pastor of New Horizons Church two years ago. After getting to know the congregation and its community, he and the leaders of the church developed a new vision statement for the future of New Horizons. All of the staff embraced the new vision except Todd, the youth director, who already had a vision statement for the youth ministry. Todd had served at the church for five years and was accustomed to operating the youth ministry independently from the rest of the congregation. Pastor Lindsey visited with Todd several times to encourage him to adapt the church's vision to the youth ministry, but Todd continued to go in his own direction. The youth group was growing and very supportive of Todd's leadership. What should Pastor Lindsey and the other leaders do?

Irreconcilable Differences?

There are occasions when Christian leaders disagree with one another over ministry styles, priorities and plans – and sometimes, as in the case of Paul and Barnabas, those disagreements can be intense!

Acts 15:36-41 describes a major dispute between these godly men as they planned their second missionary journey. Paul wanted to return to the cities that he and

Barnabas had visited on their first trip, a proposal which was fine with Barnabas. However, Barnabas wanted to include his cousin John Mark on the second journey, even though he had deserted Paul and Barnabas on their first missionary journey. Paul may have believed that John Mark was too undependable to risk taking him on the second trip. On the other hand, Barnabas, whose name means "son of encouragement," wanted to give John Mark another opportunity. He could see potential in his young cousin and wanted to invite John Mark to participate in the second journey. Barnabas enjoyed helping others grow spiritually.

At the time, both Paul and Barnabas seemed right. Paul, knowing the hardships they would encounter on their impending missionary journey, didn't want to jeopardize the trip. He needed partners he could count on. Barnabas, knowing the heart of John Mark, envisioned the kind of minister he would become (Colossians 4:10; 2 Timothy 4:11) and believed John Mark would prove himself on the next missionary journey.

Paul and Barnabas' disagreement was intense, even though it didn't involve doctrinal truth or moral issues. The Greek New Testament indicates that they had a "sharp disagreement" over John Mark (Acts 15:39).[23] Paul and Barnabas were passionate about their convictions. They would not budge, choosing instead to part ways, with Barnabas and John Mark going to Cyprus and Paul, Silas, and Timothy going to Asia Minor.

Paul and Barnabas' disagreement offers several insights into the nature of "irreconcilable differences" between spiritual leaders. First, we must regretfully acknowledge that strong disputes can occur between godly leaders. Deeply held and conflicting convictions can result in sharp disagreements, even when those convictions do not involve issues of doctrinal truth or biblical morality.

Second, while it is not sinful to disagree with other believers, Christians must not have disagreeable dispositions. This principle applies especially to church leaders since they are called to model the Christian life for believers (1 Corinthians 4:16; Hebrews 13:7). The New Testament contains numerous commands for believers to love one another (John 13:34) and lead a Spirit-filled lifestyle (Galatians 5:16-17). Christians are called to live in "newness of life," forsaking the sinful ways of their past (Romans 6:4-7) and being "kind and compassionate to one another, forgiving each other, just as in Christ God forgave you" (Ephesians 4:32).

Third, sometimes separation is preferable to ongoing disagreement. The Greek New Testament indicates that Paul and Barnabas' quarrel was continuous – neither man would accept the other's view of John Mark. Separation actually improved their witness and ultimately greatly enhanced their evangelistic outreach. As difficult as it might be to understand initially, Paul and Barnabas' separation ultimately preserved the unity of the Body of Christ.

Acts 15:36-41 does not call the irreconcilable conflict between Paul and Barnabas a sin or even a failure. It simply states that "Barnabas took Mark with him and sailed off to Cyprus. Then Paul chose Silas and departed, after being commended to the grace of the Lord by the brothers" (Acts 15:39b-40, HCSB). Later Paul invited Timothy to join his new team (Acts 16:1-5).

Five missionaries in two teams touched many more lives than three missionaries in one team would have reached. Paul embarked on a missionary journey that resulted in reaching cities that he did not plan originally to visit. He eventually established a church in the city of Philippi, and Christians throughout the centuries have been blessed by his letter to the Philippians, known as the "epistle of joy."

The Peace that Binds Us

In chapter 2, we discovered that the Bible commands us to live "with all humility and gentleness, with patience, accepting one another in love, diligently keeping the unity of the Spirit with the peace that binds us" (Ephesians 4:2-3, HCSB). Preserving or maintaining the unity of the Body of Christ through peaceful, Spirit-empowered relationships must be a priority for believers, since the health and witness of the Church is at stake.

The Apostle Paul certainly understood this truth since God had inspired him to write the Epistle to the Ephesians. Paul also wrote, "Show family affection to one another with brotherly love. Outdo one another in showing honor" (Romans 12:10, HCSB). Yet a few verses later Paul indicated that it is not always possible to maintain harmonious relationships with others: "if possible, on your part, live at peace with everyone" (Romans 12:18, HCSB).

Unfortunately, there are times when it is not possible to "live at peace" with a brother or sister in Christ, even though spiritually we are "one in Christ" (Galatians 3:28). As Paul and Barnabas discovered, sometimes the best way to preserve the unity of the Church is to part ways. Extreme care should be taken in these situations to determine God's will in the matter. We have the example of Paul and Barnabas going different directions. We also have the admonition from Paul to young Timothy, pastor of the Ephesian church, "But you, keep your head in all situations, endure hardship, do the work of an evangelist, discharge the duties of your ministry" (Ephesians 4:5). Paul's instruction was offered in the context of great persecution and conflict. The presence of conflict is an insufficient reason for leaders of a church to abandon the duties of their ministry.

All too frequently congregations force leaders to step down or leaders opt out of their duties because of the toll that conflict takes on them. No doubt churches and leaders must measure the cost of staying or going, but the decision should not be made lightly. Nor should it be made to ease the immediate pain of the conflict.

Ken Sande has offered this helpful and insightful guidance to leaders and churches:

> Although there are times when it really is best for a pastor to step down, far too many good pastors are being driven out of ministry, leaving thousands of churches weak and vulnerable to spiritual attack. Without good leadership, factions multiply, evangelism declines, divorces proceed unrestrained, discipleship loses direction, and missionaries are forgotten on the field. As Scripture warns, 'Strike the shepherd, and the sheep will be scattered' (Matt. 26:31)."[24]

Leaders who cannot reconcile their differences have an obligation to preserve the unity of their congregations, and this may mean that one or all leaders should graciously depart. However, this outcome should be the exception rather than the rule. If leaders are called to their positions by God, they should discharge the duties of their ministries until God releases them.

Who Goes, Who Stays?

In the case of Pastor Lindsey and his youth director, the solution was painfully clear. If Todd would not submit to the leadership and vision of the pastor and the other church leaders, he needed to leave the church and seek a different ministry position. The leaders of the church were united regarding the direction God was leading them. Todd's reasons for clinging to his own way could not be substantiated biblically. His heart was neither responsive nor submissive. While Todd's plans for his youth ministry were not inappropriate in themselves, the greater issue was his unrelenting rebelliousness. Had the leaders of New Horizons not handled the situation decisively and quickly, Todd could have gathered followers to join in his divisive attitudes and actions. If Todd had stayed, storm clouds would be brewing and the only horizon at New Horizons would have been dark indeed.

By staying, Pastor Lindsay could guide his congregation and help heal the wounds of conflict. He had not been in error, nor was his leadership in question. It might have been tempting for the church to ask both to leave thinking that a "clean slate" would clear the air of conflict. Yet the church would be left in an unnecessary and vulnerable position. Clearly, Todd had to leave, and Pastor Lindsay needed to stay and discharge the duties of his ministry.

Not every situation is so clear. Churches should exercise extreme caution, praying fervently before deciding who goes, who stays. God always has the answer to this question. We need to make certain we rely on His solution.

Rebellion in the Ranks

We face unprecedented division in churches of all denominations. The statistics are staggering. New churches founded in conflict are cropping up in record numbers. Fortunately, these developments do not surprise God. He has seen it all, beginning with the rebellious hearts and actions of the Israelites.

This chapter will describe many of the ways Satan's spirit of rebellion manifests itself among the people of God, offering sound scriptural principles that effectively address Satan's schemes. Christ's Church is triumphant!

Choose a New Leader

A sick, sinking feeling gripped Bob as he read the letter that arrived in the morning mail: "The following members of Bright Beginnings Church call for the pastor's resignation. We have grave concerns about his integrity and leadership methods, which cause us to be worried about the health and future of our congregation. In recent months our church has lost many longtime members, most of whom have said that they will return if he resigns. We ask that you and the other elders of Bright Beginnings Church act on our request immediately."

Bob was very familiar with the issues surrounding the pastor since the elders had spent hours investigating the firestorm of unsubstantiated allegations that had engulfed the pastor and the congregation. The church had suffered greatly as various members grumbled about the state of affairs at Bright Beginnings Church, but Bob and the other elders had sincerely believed that the worst was over. Now they knew otherwise. It was a shock to see 200 names on the petition. How should Bob and the other elders respond?

A Communicable and Deadly Disease

It's so easy to complain! When things don't go our way or don't seem right, we're tempted to grumble. The King James Version of the Bible calls this faithless activity "murmuring." Whatever it's called, grumbling is an affront to God. It reveals a disobedient and unsubmissive heart. Grumbling is deadly and destructive, harming everyone it touches.

The Israelites grumbled continuously, despite being witnesses to some of the greatest miracles recorded in the Bible. They grumbled about their thirst, hunger, monotonous diet, difficult circumstances, and leaders. Their murmuring completely exasperated Moses and brought increasingly severe punishment from God,

> And do not grumble, as some of them did - and were killed by the destroying angel.
> *1 Corinthians 10:10*

including fire from the sky, several plagues, an earthquake that swallowed complainers alive, and forty years of wandering and dying in the wilderness. On more than one occasion God simply wanted to obliterate the Israelites from the face of the earth. Had it not been for Moses' earnest intercession on behalf of the people, God would have judged Israel completely.

Grumbling played a key role in the Israelites' response to the fearful report of the eleven spies:

> That night all the people of the community raised their voices and wept aloud. All the Israelites grumbled against Moses and Aaron, and the whole assembly said to them, "If only we had died in Egypt! Or in this desert! Why is the LORD bringing us to this land only to let us fall by the sword? Our wives and children will be taken as plunder. Wouldn't it be better for us

to go back to Egypt?" And they said to each other, "We should choose a leader and go back to Egypt" (Numbers 14:1-4).

When the Israelites took their eyes off God and His promises, they succumbed to fear and disbelief. Not even Joshua and Caleb's stirring call to faith could move them to obedience (Numbers 14:7-9). Instead, the Israelites questioned God's wisdom and goodness, asking "Why is the LORD bringing us to this land only to let us fall by the sword? Our wives and children will be taken as plunder." They devised their own course of action – returning to Egypt – which foolishly overlooked the harsh realities of living as Pharaoh's slaves and revealed the prideful condition of their hearts. Most significantly, all the Israelites grumbled against their leaders (Numbers 14:2), a new development which set a precedent for nationwide complaining. It's not surprising that the people concluded their grumbling by rejecting God's appointed leaders and saying to one another, "We should choose a leader."

> Don't grumble against each other, brothers, or you will be judged. The Judge is standing at the door!
>
> James 5:9

Choosing Quick Fixes

Getting a new leader is easier than getting a new heart. Rather than repent of their lack of faith and rebellious actions, the Israelites tried to blame their leaders for their circumstances. They clamored for a quick fix by calling for a new leader who would cater to their unbelief and take them back to Egypt.

Only a small group of people sought a quick fix at Bright Beginnings Church. Determined to remove Pastor Jackson from the pulpit, they spread rumors about the pastor and told other church members that it was in everyone's "best interest" if the pastor left. They claimed that the problems at church would end once the pastor was gone. This self-appointed committee began to canvass the entire church, seeking signatures for the petition that elder Bob eventually received in the mail. Rather than resolve the problems at Bright Beginnings Church, the petition deepened existing divisions within the congregation and promoted controversy among church members.

Group Grumbling

Church members can be tempted to spiritualize grumbling and complaining by meeting to "pray" and discuss issues in small, private settings. They may attempt to legitimize their complaints by democratically voting among themselves to determine their course of action. Circumventing the Bible's admonition to speak directly to those who have offended us cannot be justified. Some members misconstrue the "honesty is best policy" cliché and speak their minds regardless of the damage they inflict. Perhaps the most devastating of all the divisive actions listed above is the ungodly practice of petitioning.

Using petitions in the church contradicts the Bible's clear teaching on conflict resolution (Matthew 18:15-17; Matthew 5:23-24) and the ways Christians should relate to one another in the Body of Christ (Romans 14:19). Petitions are inherently divisive, pitting church members against one another instead of providing for open and prayerful discussion. Rather than build consensus among church members using biblical principles, petitions employ

> Do everything without grumbling and arguing.
> *Philippians 2:14*

raw power to achieve their goals. Those who use them incorrectly assume that a majority or significant percentage of church members automatically determine God's will for a particular situation or issue (remember how all the Israelites wanted to get rid of Moses and Aaron, yet they were completely outside of God's will!). Circulating petitions can easily lead to manipulative and heavy-handed tactics which hurt innocent church members and bring disrepute on the Body of Christ. While petitions may legitimize "group grumbling" in the eyes of those who use them, God's Word is clear: "Do <u>everything</u> without grumbling and arguing" (Philippians 2:14, emphasis added).

The elders at Bright Beginnings Church wisely decided to reject the petition's call to dismiss Pastor Jackson. Instead, they used the petition as a visitation list, seeking to discover and address the signers' "grave concerns about the pastor's integrity and leadership methods." As the elders visited with each person who had signed the petition, they discovered that many people couldn't explain why they signed it. They had simply reacted emotionally to the problems in the church. Some who had signed the petition were personal friends of those who were seeking the pastor's dismissal. Many were inactive or minimally involved in the life of the congregation. Others had been pressured to sign the petition. A few were not even members of Bright Beginnings Church!

The once formidable petition was now reduced to a short list of unhappy and controlling individuals who didn't care who they hurt or how they damaged the cause of Christ as they attempted to force their will on the congregation. The elders of Bright Beginnings Church discovered the truth and preserved the unity of the congregation by graciously and prayerfully visiting those who had signed the petition. Rather than succumb to the petition's demands or react defensively and lash out at the "troublemakers" in the church, the elders' response strengthened the congregation and set the proper context for the discipline of divisive church members.

Before you quickly assume that your church needs a new leader, ask yourself the following questions:

- Did I vote to call the pastor believing then he was God's man for our church?

- Is the pastor's doctrine or leadership style contrary to the Bible?

- Do I pray for my pastor every day?

- Do I consistently seek to help the pastor strengthen his ministry by being a support to him?

- Do I minister to the needs of my pastor and his family?

As noted earlier in this book, there are times when a congregation must ask its pastor to resign and choose a new leader. However, this happens far more often than it should in churches of all denominations. Seeking a new leader is easier than addressing rebellious hearts and ways. When the path of least resistance is taken and a congregation focuses on "choosing a new leader" instead of addressing its unhealthy spiritual condition, it is only a matter of time until conflict will rear its ugly head and further mar the beauty of the Bride of Christ, the Church.

Wolves Among You

A wolf pack can kill dozens of sheep in a single night, leaving half-consumed carcasses strewn about as grim evidence of the rampage. Rather than kill their prey quickly, wolves literally eat their victims alive until they become interested in their next opportunity. Wolves are cunning, capable, and ferocious.

Sheep, on the other hand, are gentle creatures that are oblivious to the dangers around them. They are completely dependent on their caretakers. Sheep need shepherds to protect them from wolves and other predators.

Wolves in Sheep's Clothing

Jesus used sheep and wolves to describe the relationship between His followers and those who seek to harm them. He said, "I am the good shepherd; I know my sheep and my sheep know me" (John 10:14). Because Jesus loves His followers and understood the dangers that constantly threatened them, He said, "Watch out for false prophets. They come to you in sheep's clothing, but inwardly they are ferocious wolves" (Matthew 7:15). Appearances can be deceiving as well as deadly, then and today.

Pastor Ed clearly remembered the Sunday when a particular woman joined Saint's Haven Congregation. Barbara radiated joy, enthusiasm, and confidence and was eager to become a Bible teacher. She was a refreshing change for Ed, since most new members were reluctant to become involved in ministry. Also, teachers were in short supply.

I [Paul] know that after my departure savage wolves will come in among you, not sparing the flock. And men from among yourselves will rise up with deviant doctrines to lure the disciples into following them. Therefore be on the alert.
Acts 20:29-31a. HCSB

Four weeks after Barbara joined the church, Pastor Ed asked her to lead a Bible study. She was delighted to accept his invitation and quickly began recruiting class members from the congregation.

At first, Ed received glowing reports from the people in Barbara's study. Within months, very disturbing reports started trickling in as one member after another described her extremely assertive ways, how she demanded the allegiance of class members and became unusually involved in their personal lives. Apparently, someone less than saintly had crept into the Haven's safe sanctuary.

We tend to recall extreme examples when we think of recent false teachers, men such as Jim Jones or David Koresh who advocated bizarre doctrines and horrific practices. Since their evil intent was obvious, even the secular press correctly identified them as cultists. Most false teachers, however, are much more subtle in their approach. As Pastor Ed discovered, we can welcome false teachers into our churches with open arms, becoming aware of their true identity only after they have begun to wreak havoc in our congregations.

How can we avoid this heart-wrenching experience? The Bible helps us identify false teachers by exposing many of their motives, methods, and messages.

The Motives of Deceivers

In order to understand the motives of false teachers, we must be aware of the relationship between them and the ultimate father of lies, Satan. The Apostle Paul called them Satan's "servants," noting that

> such people are false apostles, deceitful workers, disguising themselves as apostles of Christ. And no wonder! For Satan himself is disguised as an angel of light. So it is no great thing if his servants also disguise themselves as servants of righteousness. Their destiny will be according to their works (2 Corinthians 11:13-15, HCSB).

Not every false teacher appears greedy, especially at first, but he or she is intrinsically motivated by selfish interests. False teachers are not interested in building up the Body of Christ through selfless and sacrificial service. Instead, they are motivated by what they can gain through the ways they influence a local congregation. False teachers "do not serve our Lord Christ but their own appetites" (Romans 16:18, HCSB).

Not all false teachers advocate blatant sexual immorality (Jude 7-8), but their values will be shaped by the world's values. False teachers lead others into sin using worldly standards to rationalize godless behavior. They might use biblical terminology, but the practical outcomes of their teaching turn grace into a pretext for sin.

False teachers are driven by the forces that motivate Satan: pride, ambition, power, control, and indulgence. Like their master, they attempt to entice unsuspecting church members into foolishly believing that they can "be like God" (Genesis 3:5) and disregard His rightful claim on their lives as the King of the universe.

Some of the major false teachings infiltrating our churches today include:

- There are many paths to heaven

- We cannot judge others

- Politics and religion don't mix

- Women have the right to choose abortion

- Homosexuality is not sin; it is an acceptable lifestyle

- The Bible is unreliable, filled with errors

- Spirituality can replace a relationship with Christ

- Absolute truth does not exist; truth is relative

- Faith is personal and private; it should not be shared with other people

The Methods of Deceivers

False teachers "will secretly introduce destructive heresies" to a congregation (2 Peter 2:1). They enter churches "secretly" (Jude 4), and "flatter others" to "deceive the hearts of the unsuspecting" (Romans 16:18, HCSB).

False teachers are "idle talkers" (Titus 1:10, HCSB). They frequently have big plans and exciting ideas that lack spiritual substance. Their proposals catch the attention of church members but slowly lead them away from the basic disciplines of the Christian life and faithful service in the church.

False teachers are divisive. The Apostle Paul understood how damaging their presence can be to the Body of Christ. He wrote, "I urge you, brothers, to watch out for those who cause divisions....Keep away from them" (Romans 16:17). They grumble and find fault (Jude 16), creating strife and division among believers (Jude 19).

Finally, false teachers distort scripture. Referring to the Apostle Paul's epistles, Peter observed that "the untaught and unstable twist them to their own destruction, as they also do with the rest of the Scriptures" (2 Peter 3:16, HCSB). Truth becomes blurred and impotent when mixed with falsehood. During His earthly ministry, Jesus strongly rebuked false teachers, saying, "You are in error because you do not know the Scriptures or the power of God" (Matthew 22:29).

The Messages of Deceivers

Word about Barbara's disturbing teaching spread like wildfire through the membership of Saint's Haven Congregation. One Sunday she questioned the inspiration and reliability of the Gospels, telling class members that modern scholarship had proven long ago that the Gospels contain

*numerous discrepancies. "Because of this," Barbara declared
authoritatively, "we cannot know with certainty what Jesus
actually did and said. All we know is what various people wrote
long after Jesus walked on the earth. Our New Testament
reflects their beliefs, not historical facts and events."*

*When class members told her they had not heard this before,
Barbara questioned Pastor Ed's theological training. She even
suggested that he might be deliberately withholding the truth
about the Bible from the congregation. Class members were
bewildered and upset, wondering if Barbara's accusations about
the pastor might be true.*

False teachers blaspheme spiritual realities (Jude 8),
enslaving themselves and others to darkened thinking and
sinful lifestyles. In the early church, they sought to change
the truth about salvation (read Acts 15 and the Book of
Galatians to learn more about their legalistic approach to
salvation). Later, other false teachers blatantly denied "the
sovereign Lord who bought them" (2 Peter 2:1). False
teachers often will add or subtract to the basic biblical
truths about Christ, creating "a different gospel"
(Galatians 1:6) that is not really the gospel at all. Satan and
his servants will do anything in their power to keep people
from being saved.

Our Shepherd Will Protect His Sheep

Unfortunately, there are many false teachers and
deceivers who are attempting to destroy churches and
keep people from experiencing saving faith through Jesus
Christ (Titus 1:10). They possess "a form of godliness but
[deny] its power" (2 Timothy 3:5). However, they "will
[bring] swift destruction on themselves" (2 Peter 2:1).
Their judgment is certain (2 Peter 2:3) since the "gloom of
darkness has been reserved for them" (2 Peter 2:17, HCSB).

We should be encouraged and emboldened by what John MacArthur has written regarding sheep, wolves and the Good Shepherd:

> We are sheep among wolves. It was not uncommon in Palestine to hear about a shepherd found dead among the sheep he was trying to defend. But our Shepherd is not dead – He ever lives and is our defender. There is an invincibility about us because He controls everything. Zechariah 2:8 says, "He that toucheth you toucheth the apple of his eye." If you think it's tough on the sheep, it will be tougher on the wolves for what they do to the sheep. God will make all things right in the end. No matter what Satan does, he can't destroy God's sheep.[25]

Jesus said, "My sheep listen to my voice; I know them; and they follow me. I give them eternal life; and they shall never perish; no one can snatch them out of my hand" (John 10:27-28). Our Shepherd will protect His sheep!

The Spirit of Jezebel

Just mention the name Jezebel and people think of an evil, conniving, strong-willed woman. Her name has become synonymous with evil, so much so that many people who haven't read the Bible know it's not flattering to be called a "Jezebel."

The Original Jezebel

Jezebel was born in the Phoenician city of Sidon, located north of Israel in modern-day Lebanon. She was the daughter of King Ethbaal, whose name honored the god Baal. Jezebel became a zealous advocate of Baal worship which sought, among other things, to ensure the change of seasons and bountiful harvests. Devotees sought to influence Baal and other gods for their personal gain and prosperity, combining religion, economics and gross immorality in their worship.

King Ahab of Israel married Jezebel for political and commercial reasons, entering into an unholy alliance with the Phoenicians. When Jezebel became queen, Ahab built a dazzling temple for Baal in his capital city of Samaria. There Ahab "proceeded to serve Baal and worship him" (1 Kings 16:31, HCSB). Ahab willingly compromised his faith and violated God's commands in order to bring security and prosperity to Israel.

> Ahab did more to provoke the LORD God of Israel than all the kings who were before him.
> *1 Kings 16:33b*

Jezebel's name literally means "un-husbanded." Although she was married to Ahab, she refused to submit to his leadership as a husband or king. Jezebel became the dominate force in Israel's religious, political and social life. She lured her husband into Baal worship (1 Kings 16:31-33), established false prophets for Baal throughout the land (1 Kings 18:19), slaughtered most of God's prophets (1 Kings 18:4), completely demoralized Elijah with her threat to kill him (1 Kings 19:2), orchestrated a plot to kill an innocent man, Naboth, to get his vineyard for Ahab (1 Kings 19:21), and constantly encouraged Ahab "to do what was evil in the LORD's sight" (1 Kings 21:25, HCSB).

Following Ahab's death, Jezebel influenced Israel for fourteen years, both personally and through her family. It took a direct command from God and a military coup to end her demonic hold on Israel (2 Kings 9). Until she met her divinely appointed demise (2 Kings 9:30-37), Satan used her to advance his unholy purposes among God's people.

Jezebel's Spirit Is Alive and Well

The spirit embodied by Jezebel continues to flourish in many congregations today. Her domineering, manipulating, and destructive ways are evident in the lives of men and women who have given Satan a foothold in their lives. John Franklin and Chuck Lawless have written that the word "foothold" can be "translated as 'opportunity' (NASB) or place (KJV). [The word] literally means 'space.' Hence Christians are to be careful not to give the devil any space in their lives."[26]

Disobedient church members can deliberately or unwittingly display some of the qualities of a Jezebel spirit. Their words and actions tear down the Body of Christ, discourage other believers and hamper the progress of the gospel. Sometimes members of satanic groups infiltrate churches in order to create as much disruption and division as possible. Like Jezebel's efforts to destroy Elijah and the other prophets of God, they seek the downfall of pastors and other church leaders.

Word spread among the Sunday School classes of Devoted Disciples Fellowship about a special prayer meeting that would be held at a church member's home. The meeting was called to pray for the growing unrest in the church.

The man who was organizing the meeting had been a member of the church for about a year. Antonio exuded an air of confidence and had been given several influential positions within the congregation, including being a teacher and a member of the church council. People looked to him for answers, and he was more than willing to offer his views.

Antonio didn't invite the pastor, elders or members of the personnel committee to the meeting. As the meeting began, Antonio reviewed the complaints and "concerns" he had heard about the pastor. All eyes were glued on him. He declared, "We've got to do something about this situation. The pastor has to go!"

Those who embody the spirit of Jezebel delight to incite rebellion among the ranks of a congregation. They take specific pleasure in targeting and destroying God's anointed. Because these individuals can exact heavy damage, often ruining the ministry of spiritual leaders, it is imperative that churches confront these destructive forces before great damage is done.

How Jezebel Enters Your Church

Satan knows that spiritual compromise, moral failure, a lack of discernment, and passive leadership offer him windows of opportunity to attack congregations. The Jezebel spirit quickly exploits these weaknesses to accomplish its demonic goals in churches.

Dale, a longtime deacon in a church, told his young, new pastor that most of the problems they had experienced in their church were initiated by strong, controlling women. During one church conflict, deacons' wives had been particularly problematic. They didn't like the way their husbands were handling a church issue, so they took matters in their hands and escalated the conflict. Dale further shared that one women's class consistently stirred up dissension and frequently went to war over decisions the pastor made.

When asked if these problems were resolved, Dale looked down and quietly responded, "No." The young pastor knew conflict with these women was only a matter of time. He immediately began praying for wisdom, discernment and strength for the battle that was certain to come.

Spiritual Compromise

One of Ahab's great failures was his indifference to the

truth. He knew that God had clearly instructed His people not to intermarry with foreigners. Such marriages would compromise the Israelites' obedience to God. Yet Ahab valued national security and economic gain more than spiritual faithfulness, and he and Israel suffered greatly because of his decision to marry Jezebel.

> You must not intermarry with [foreign women], because they will surely turn your hearts after their gods.
> *1 Kings 11:2*

Like many people today, Ahab wanted the "best" of both worlds. On the one hand, he married Jezebel and became an active worshiper of Baal (1 Kings 16:31); on the other hand, he vainly attempted to retain vestiges of his faith in God by how he named two of his children: Ahaziah means "Yahweh sustains" and Joram is translated "Yahweh is exalted." He put Obediah, a devout believer in the Lord, in charge of his palace (1 Kings 18:3) and summoned Obediah for assistance during a severe famine (1 Kings 18:2-3). He frequently surrounded himself with prophets to look spiritual, but he didn't heed their advice and grew irritable when they corrected him.

God's verdict on Ahab's spiritual compromise was clear. 1 Kings 21:25 summarizes Ahab's life by recording that "there was no one like Ahab, who devoted himself to do what was evil in the LORD's sight, because his wife Jezebel incited him" (HCSB).

Lest we make the mistake of believing that we cannot compromise spiritually, we should remember Christ's judgment on the church at Thyatira: "...I have this against you: You tolerate that woman Jezebel, who calls herself a prophetess. By her teaching she misleads my servants into sexual immorality and the eating of food sacrificed to idols" (Revelation 2:20).

Like Ahab, Christians in Thyatira compromised their faith for personal security and economic prosperity. The

"Jezebel" at Thyatira apparently encouraged believers to protect their business interests by participating in the pagan worship activities of various trade guilds.[27] Spiritual compromise occurs whenever we value something more highly than our relationship with God.

The consequences of compromise for us can be severe, just as they were for Ahab and the nation of Israel. The church of Thyatira received Christ's righteous judgment for its compromise: "Look! I will throw [Jezebel] into a sickbed, and those who commit adultery with her into great tribulation, unless they repent of her practices. I will kill her children with the plague. Then all the churches will know that I am the One who examines minds and hearts, and I will give to each of you according to your works" (Revelation 2:22-23, HCSB). Another example of judgment for compromise is found after the Apostle Paul admonished believers to examine themselves as part of the Lord's Supper: "whoever eats the bread or drinks the cup of the Lord in an unworthy way will be guilty of sin against the body and blood of the Lord. This is why many are sick and ill among you, and many have fallen asleep" (1 Corinthians 11:27,30).

Moral Failure

The spirit of Jezebel can enter your church when leaders and members fail to guard themselves against sexual immorality. Jezebel is a temptress and uses every means available to lure believers away from God (Revelation 2:20). More than one congregation has experienced great difficulties due to the sexual allure of a Jezebel in its midst. Church leaders are especially vulnerable to this kind of attack since Satan knows the damage that can be done to the cause of Christ when a leader falls into immorality.

Lack of Discernment

Because Ahab compromised himself spiritually, he lacked the discernment necessary to avoid marrying Jezebel. One sin naturally led to even greater sin, even though Ahab was blind to his downward spiral. As Proverbs 12:15a says, "A fool's way is right in his own eyes" (HCSB).

Some church leaders lack the spiritual gift of discernment. Unlike Ahab, this deficiency is not due to any sin on their part but to the way God has uniquely gifted them. Pastors and other church leaders need a high degree of discernment to lead their congregations, especially when dealing with Jezebel spirits. If leaders lack this level of discernment, they need to acknowledge their deficiency and seek the counsel of godly church members who are gifted spiritually to "test the spirits."

> Dear friends, do not believe every spirit, but test the spirits to see whether they are from God, because many false prophets have gone out into the world.
> *1 John 4:1*

Passive Leadership

One of Ahab's faults was his passive approach to leadership. Simply stated, he was not the leader of his home or kingdom. Instead, he abdicated his authority and allowed Jezebel to set the agenda for his life and kingship. This critical weakness is portrayed in the account of Naboth's vineyard, which shows Jezebel's domination and manipulation of Ahab (1 Kings 21:1-7) and her deceitful, murderous ways (1 Kings 21:8-16).

Passive church leaders endanger their ministry and congregations. Engaging a Jezebel spirit is difficult and some leaders choose to avoid the unpleasant experience of confrontation. If they truly care for their congregation and desire Christ's approval, they must confront a Jezebel spirit using biblical guidelines and much prayer.

Pause to pray for your leaders. Consider praying for:

- Wisdom and discernment to perceive the presence of those who embody the Jezebel spirit

- Godly prayer partners to support and help hold the pastor accountable for shepherding and protecting the flock

- The Holy Spirit's empowerment in your pastor's preaching, so he will boldly proclaim God's truth – regardless of opposition

- Workers who are godly, committed, and supportive to come alongside the pastor and help him build up the church

- Strong relationships between the church staff to keep disagreements from becoming destructive or divisive

- The families of church staff

- All individuals in positions of leadership - that their ministries will flourish and the Kingdom will be advanced through them

The Care and Feeding of Troublemakers

> A passerby who meddles in a quarrel that's not his is like one who grabs a dog by the ears (Proverbs 26:17, HCSB).

We might chuckle over this pearl of "down home" godly wisdom, but it's not a laughing matter when we become involved in a quarrel between church members.

Grabbing a dog by the ears is hazardous! However, there are times when we must intervene in disputes between church members in order to "keep the unity of the Spirit through the bond of peace" (Ephesians 4:3).

The unfortunate reality is that many congregations have more than one troublemaker in their midst, people who are chronically disagreeable and contentious. Whether bitter over circumstances in life or difficult since birth, troublemakers create one problem after another in churches. They're not false teachers or evil Jezebels, they're just unhappy people! Not only that, many times they seem to make it their mission in life to make others miserable and unhappy.

A leader in the largest Protestant denomination in the United States summed up his experience with congregations by saying, "There are not many happy churches," he observed. "Most churches are struggling, arguing, fighting, firing a pastor, hiring a pastor. Here we are dealing with all of this while the world is unraveling around us."[28]

Troublemakers are rarely concerned about the spiritual condition of the world. They're typically the first to vote "no" at a church business meeting, seldom engage in ministry to others, and often give very little financially to their churches. Yet they feel entitled to insist on their way even when they hurt other people and harm the Body of Christ.

It should come as no surprise that troublemakers are not committed to building up the Body of Christ. Their interests are inherently self-centered and their actions are always sinful and destructive.

Types of Troublemakers

Bible Bloviators

A host for a cable news network program used to urge his viewers not to "bloviate" when sending him emails.[29] To "bloviate" means "to discourse at length in a pompous or boastful manner."[30] Less bloviating would improve the spiritual climate of our churches! After beautifully describing our amazing salvation in Christ (Titus 3:3-7), Paul gave Titus the following instructions:

> And I want you to stress these things, so that those who have trusted in God may be careful to devote themselves to doing what is good. These things are excellent and profitable for everyone. But avoid foolish controversies and genealogies and arguments and quarrels about the law, because these are unprofitable and useless (Titus 3:8-9).

Paul urged Titus to focus on the "basics" of the Christian life, avoiding the temptation to get caught up in foolish arguments over the Jewish law, which didn't lead to salvation or godliness. We must focus on teaching and sharing the basics about salvation through Jesus Christ and living the Christian life. This is what our Lord had in mind when he gave us the Great Commission: "Go, therefore, and make disciples of all nations" (Matthew 28:19a, HCSB). Disciplemaking, not bloviating, will accomplish our mission as the Church of Jesus Christ!

Bitter Brawlers

A second category of church troublemakers includes those who have a bitter spirit. Their bitterness can come from unresolved hurtful experiences inside or outside the church. As Kent Crockett has observed, "Bitterness is the offspring of an unhealed wound – whose parents are unforgiveness and time."[31]

Frustrated over being unable to change the past, bitter people choose prisons of their own making and refuse to change their hearts. Consequently, they frequently lash out and hurt the people around them.

The Book of Hebrews instructs us to engage in peacemaking as a lifestyle and avoid the infectious poison of bitterness:

> Pursue peace with everyone, and holiness – without it no one will see the Lord. See to it that no one falls short of the grace of God and that no root of bitterness springs up, causing trouble and by it, defiling many (Hebrews 12:14-15, HCSB).

Every believer must "see to it...that no root of bitterness springs up" beginning with his or her own heart. Most roots are hidden beneath the ground, but given the right conditions they can sprout suddenly and develop into a plant or tree. In the same way, bitterness can emerge from a person's heart with serious consequences to the spiritual health of a congregation. Bitterness is a highly contagious disease, spreading quickly and harming the unity, fellowship, and evangelistic impact of the Body of Christ.

If you harbor a bitter spirit, relinquish it to the Lord. Forgive those who have hurt you, offering them the same grace that you received through Jesus Christ. You cannot change the past and you cannot force others to change, but you can open yourself to be transformed through the power of God in your life.

Chronic Complainers

Complaining displays a lack of faith in God's power, provision, and promises. It also shows a complete disregard for the spiritual welfare of others in the Body of Christ. It does not build up others and is discouraging.

As we discovered in chapters 2 and 3 of this book, the people of Israel complained continuously even though they had experienced God's direct intervention on their behalf on numerous occasions. Complaining didn't help them, and it won't help us! Instead of complaining, start praying. If another Christian begins to complain, take that person aside and pray for him or her. Remind your brother or sister in Christ that chronic complaining is harmful spiritually. Most importantly, tell them that God is greatly displeased by complaining.

When someone begins to complain, show them the passage below. Note how we are tempted to feel like the Israelites when difficult circumstances come our way. Then, like the prophet Isaiah, direct them to the amazing resources that are available to all who believe and trust in God.

> Why do you say, O Jacob, and complain, O Israel, "My way is hidden from the LORD; my cause is disregarded by my God?" Do you not know? Have you not heard? The LORD is the everlasting God, the Creator of the ends of the earth. He will not grow tired or weary, and his understanding no one can fathom. He gives strength to the weary and increases the power of the weak. Even youths grow tired and weary, and young men stumble and fall; but those who hope in the LORD will renew their strength. They will soar on wings like eagles;

they will run and not grow weary, they will walk and not be faint (Isaiah 40:27-31).

Gloating Gossips

We don't have to repeat everything we've heard. As a matter of fact, we shouldn't! There's a good chance that what we've heard isn't accurate since gossip is inherently unreliable. And if what we've heard is true, we still shouldn't repeat it. We shouldn't even listen to it.

Gossip involves demeaning a person in their absence in a way that damages his or her reputation. It prejudices other people against that person without his or her knowledge and does not give him or her an opportunity to respond to the rumors. Gossip spreads like wildfire and takes a tremendous toll on its victims.

> No rotten talk should come from your mouth, but only what is good for the building up of someone in need, in order to give grace to those who hear.
> *Ephesians 4:29*

The Bible commands us to "pursue what promotes peace and what builds up one another" (Romans 14:19, HCSB). Gossip can't do these things. Instead, it betrays confidences (Proverbs 11:13), hurts deeply (Proverbs 26:22), and separates close friends (Proverbs 16: 28). The Apostle Paul included it in a list of sins that most Christians wouldn't dream of committing: "quarreling, jealousy, outbursts of anger, selfish ambitions, slander, gossip, arrogance, and disorder" (2 Corinthians 12:20, HCSB). Yet far too many church members routinely sin by gossiping.

Given the fact that gossip is destructive and commonplace, why do so many professing Christians continue to do it? One reason is simple. It's extremely easy to gossip. Another reason is that there's usually very little, if any, immediate accountability. Very few Christians, including pastors and church leaders, undertake the unpleasant task of confronting a gossip. However, God's standard is high and uncompromising: "No rotten talk should come from your mouth" (Ephesians 4:29, HCSB, emphasis added). This command includes gossip.

Jealous Jabbers

You can spot jealous jabbers easily; they are green – green with envy. But they are careful to shade their green eyes with dark glasses of false spirituality. Underneath those dark glasses their eyes are constantly roaming to see what others are doing and what others are getting. They look for who's getting the recognition or funding for their ministry. They constantly question, "Why is she getting to serve on that committee?" or "Why does he get the funds needed for his program?" If left unchecked, these jealous feelings poison a person's heart.

The Bible states that jealous hearts soon ooze deadly venom to the tongue: "They were filled with jealousy and talked abusively against what Paul was saying" (Acts 13:45b). "For since there is jealousy and quarreling among you, are you not worldly? Are you not acting like mere men?" (1 Corinthians 3:3b)

The Care and Feeding of Troublemakers

Troublemakers take an extraordinary amount of time and attention away from a pastor's biblical priorities in ministry. They reduce his effectiveness and make his ministry unnecessarily complicated and unpleasant. Regrettably, troublemakers are a fact of congregational life. With the full support and participation of the other leaders in the church, the pastor must prayerfully and courageously confront troublemakers so that they will not continue to wreak havoc among God's people. The pastor and church leaders must remember Paul's instructions to Timothy as they deal with troublemakers in the church:

> And the Lord's servant must not quarrel; instead, he must be kind to everyone, able to teach, not resentful. Those who oppose him he must gently instruct, in the hope that God will grant them repentance leading them to a knowledge of the truth, and that they will come to their senses and escape from the trap of the devil, who has taken them captive to do his will (2 Timothy 2:24-26).

Paul gave specific instructions on how to deal with unrepentant troublemakers: "Warn a divisive person once, and then warn him a second time. After that, have nothing to do with him. You may be sure that such a man is warped and sinful; he is self-condemned" (Titus 3:10-11). Strong words indeed, but the stakes are high. People need the Lord, and our churches must focus on reaching them!

On Sheep and Shepherding

Rebellion in the ranks of church members happens frequently in congregations due to the presence of false teachers, Jezebel spirits and troublemakers. Misunderstanding regarding the pastor's role and responsibilities is another reason why churches experience conflict.

The pastor is the shepherd of a congregation. The Greek word for pastor is *poimen* which literally means "shepherd." In his book, *Being Leaders*, Aubrey Malphurs describes how many churches view the role and responsibilities of a pastor in a way that originated with the Puritans in New England. They considered pastors to be "physician[s] of the soul" whose primary responsibilities entailed the pastoral care of church members.[32]

Malphurs writes that this approach to the pastor's role and responsibilities misunderstands "what shepherds did in biblical times. It assumes that a shepherd spent most of his day taking care of sheep, but it is more accurate to think of a shepherd as a sheep leader than a sheep caregiver."[33] A pastor/shepherd is the leader of the flock, ensuring its well-being through his leadership and protection. A pastor follows the shepherding example set by God: "The LORD is my shepherd...he <u>leads</u> me beside quiet waters...he <u>guides</u> me in paths of righteousness" (Psalm 23:1-3, emphasis added).

Other Old Testament passages make a clear connection between shepherding and leading. God said to David, "You will shepherd My people Israel and be ruler over Israel" (2 Samuel 5:2; see also 2 Samuel 7:7). In the New Testament, those who are called to serve as pastors of local congregations govern (Romans 12:6,8), direct (1 Timothy 5:17), and protect their people (Acts 20:28; see also 1 Peter 5:1-2).

These passages clearly indicate that a pastor serves his congregation by leading it. Unfortunately, many churches don't want their pastor to be their leader. They prefer a chaplain who cares for them personally, not a leader who guides them according to his God-given vision for the future.

> Obey your leaders and submit to them, for they keep watch over your souls.
> *Hebrews 13:17a, HCSB*

How do you view your pastor? Review the following list of pastoral expectations to determine which ones are truly biblical. Then consider if you impose any unscriptural or unrealistic expectations on your pastor.

- He should be our family chaplain helping us through

major crises in life

- He should be my spiritual leader, challenging me to a closer personal walk with God

- He should help me grow spiritually even when it involves correction

- He should always visit me and others when we are in the hospital

- He should be available to me any time I need him

- He should establish the vision for our church and lead us there even if it means personal and church-wide change

- He should attend our important family celebrations

- He should oversee all the maintenance of the church building

Based upon his extensive experience as a church consultant and researcher, Aubrey Malphurs has observed that church members are at various stages in their responsiveness to a pastor's leadership.[34] "Early followers" respond favorably to a new pastor, usually within the first year of his pastorate. "Middle followers" are open to following a new pastor but take two to six years to develop confidence in his leadership. "Late followers" need up to eight years to trust a new pastor, often because they must process negative experiences from the past. A troublesome minority of church members can be labeled "never followers" because they refuse to follow any pastor's leadership under any circumstances.

If you were present when your pastor arrived at your church, evaluate how you have followed him since that time.

- I was an "early follower"

- I was a "middle follower"

- I was a "late follower"

- I am a "never follower"

Your pastor and the other church leaders need your support, and you need their support and guidance. If your leaders were called by the church to the positions in which they serve, they deserve double honor by the congregation (1 Timothy 5:17).

Most church members have little knowledge about a pastor or staff member's daily activities. When we don't know something, we usually assume the worst. Determine now to assume the best of your pastor and church leaders. Their job is difficult because they operate as an opposing force to the darkness in our world. They put on the armor of God daily and go out to defend the cause of Christ and His church. Help your leaders, pray for them, and make it a joy for them to serve you! The more help you offer your leaders, the more you will see how much they do for your church.

Matters of the Heart

We must follow God's Word in order to resolve conflict in ways that will glorify Him and build up the Body of Christ. God always begins with the heart. As we submit to Christ's lordship over our lives and churches and surrender our agendas to advance God's kingdom, we will possess the ability to love others with God's redeeming love, to conduct ourselves in difficult situations according to God's wisdom, and to trust God's truth, methods and timing. This chapter will focus on the heart of a peacemaking Christian.

Sweet Surrender

Joann couldn't get over the hurt she felt as she recalled the way she had been removed as the president of the women's fellowship at Serenity Heights Church. Rather than follow the usual procedure for electing new officers at the end of the year, someone in the group had called every woman except Joann, inviting members to come to the next regularly scheduled meeting an hour early in order to conduct some urgent business. That "business" was Joann. Another woman was elected unanimously to replace Joann as president. When Joann arrived for the meeting, the new president informed her of the group's decision in a cold, matter-of-fact manner, without offering an explanation or words of appreciation.

Joann was crushed. She called several of the women in the days that followed the meeting, but no one would answer her questions. They seemed to avoid her, even on Sundays. Joann felt shunned and shamed.

She didn't know why the group had rejected her, but she knew that they had not treated her fairly. Their actions were inexcusable. How could she discover the truth about what had happened? Why were her sisters in Christ treating her so cruelly?

Jesus Is Lord!

The bold declaration "Jesus is Lord" empowered the early Christians and transformed the world. Peter concluded his Spirit-filled sermon on the day of Pentecost by saying, "Therefore let all the house of Israel know with certainty that God has made this Jesus, whom you crucified, both Lord and Messiah" (Acts 2:36, HCSB). The Apostle Paul wrote, "This is the message of faith that we proclaim: if you confess with your mouth, 'Jesus is Lord,' and believe in your heart that God raised Him from the dead, you will be saved" (Romans 10:8b-9, HCSB). In Philippians 2:5-11, Paul described Christ's humility and exaltation by writing that "at the name of Jesus every knee should bow, in heaven and on earth and under the earth, and every tongue confess that Jesus Christ is Lord, to the glory of God the Father" (Philippians 2:10-11).

Jesus is Lord! He is Lord whether or not we acknowledge His lordship. As the second person of the Trinity and the One who triumphed over death through the power of God, Jesus stands victorious over everything in creation, including our sin and rebellion. One day every knee will bow to Him and acknowledge His lordship. He was and is and will forever be the "Lord of lords and King of kings" (Revelation 17:14).

Jesus' disciples watched with amazement as He demonstrated His lordship by turning water into wine (John 2:1-12), healing the sick and afflicted (Matthew 8:5-13), liberating the demon-possessed (Matthew 8:28-34), calming storms (Matthew 8:23-27; Matthew 15:21-28), forgiving sin (Matthew 9:2; Luke 7:48), and raising the dead (Luke 7:11-15; John 11:1-44). Jesus also proclaimed His lordship through His preaching and teaching (Luke

4:18-19). Most significantly, Jesus displayed His lordship with power and authority through His resurrection. As doubting Thomas examined the wounds of the resurrected Savior, he confessed Jesus' lordship by exclaiming, "My Lord and my God!" (John 20:28)

Jesus Is Lord of Your Life

Jesus is Lord of your life. He deserves your best and all, and He calls you to be His fully devoted follower. As the Apostle Paul wrote in Colossians 2:6, "just as you received Christ Jesus as Lord, continue to live in him." There is incredible power available to believers who submit their lives to the lordship of Jesus Christ.

Assess your degree of surrender to Christ's lordship by determining if the following statements apply to your life:

- Jesus is lord over my finances

- Jesus is lord over my body – health and holiness

- Jesus is lord over my relationships

- Jesus is lord over my failures

- Jesus is lord over my successes

- Jesus is lord over my time and agenda

- Jesus is lord over my priorities

- Jesus is lord over my future

- Jesus is lord over me – my heart, all that I am

Surrendering to the lordship of Jesus Christ is a life-long process of spiritual growth to maturity. As John Piper has observed, "the lordship of Christ, in reality, is something that is not discovered and yielded to once, but thousands of times."[35]

Jesus Is Lord of Your Church

Reflect on the Apostle John's amazing vision of Jesus as He walked among the seven churches of the Book of Revelation (Revelation 2:1–3:22). John writes,

> Among the lampstands [e.g., the seven churches] was someone "like a son of man," dressed in a robe reaching down to his feet and with a golden sash around his chest. His head and hair were white like wool, as white as snow, and his eyes were like blazing fire. His feet were like bronze glowing in a furnace, and his voice was like the sound of rushing waters. In his right hand he held seven stars, and out of his mouth came a sharp double-edged sword. His face was like the sun shining in all its brilliance (Revelation 1:13-16).

John was overwhelmed by the Lord of lords: "When I saw him, I fell at his feet as though dead" (Revelation 1:17a). The same Lord walks among the members of your church, bringing words of encouragement and righteous judgment. As Jesus knew the seven churches of Revelation, so He knows your church (Revelation 2:2; 2:9; 2:13; 2:19; 3:1; 3:8; 3:15). His eyes see everything, and you can trust Him to judge, cleanse and correct that which is sinful in your church. As the Head of His Church (Ephesians 4:15; 5:23; Colossians 1:18; 2:19), Christ is vitally interested in the health and welfare of His Body.

No matter how difficult circumstances might be in your church, trust the Lord of the Church, Jesus, to take care of His Bride. Relinquish the desire to take matters into your own hands. Hear His words to your congregation by reading, believing and praying scripture. Then declare His Word lovingly yet boldly, so that He can work miracles in your congregation.

The ladies in the women's fellowship never explained the reasons behind their decision to Joann. She struggled with her feelings for two months, at times almost frantic for an answer, for resolution.

One day while crying out to the Lord in anguish, she felt a push of conviction from the Holy Spirit. She knew she had to give up the need to control the situation. She knew she had to trust God for the outcome, patiently waiting for love to win them over. Through her tears she whispered, "God I just give this up to you. Don't let me take it back. Deal with their hearts and deal with mine. Make me holy and I'll leave them up to you."

Jesus is Lord of your life and church. He is Lord of everything, including your hurt, questions, worries, and failures. Instead of harboring these destructive forces in your heart, surrender them to the Lord. Give them up, relinquishing control of them and asking Jesus to address your concerns.

Henry Blackaby offers powerful insight on letting God uphold our integrity when we have been wronged or misunderstood by others.

> At times, God will be the only witness to your righteous behavior.... When no one seems to understand why you have done something or when others question whether you have done all you should have done, your confidence should not be in the hope of vindication in the eyes of others. It should be in the knowledge that God keeps you in His sight. If you have this confidence, it will be enough to sustain you.[36]

Jesus Is Lord over Those Who Have Wronged You

In surrendering her hurt and need for vindication, Joann surrendered her heart to the lordship of Christ. She could have spent years asking "why" and longing for her integrity to be restored in the eyes of those who wronged her. Instead her release brought freedom. She could move on to serve the Lord wherever He called her. Although the ladies who wronged Joann never asked for her forgiveness, Joann could forgive them in her heart. In doing so, she filled her heart with Christ's compassion. She could genuinely pray for those who had failed her.

Take comfort in the truth that Jesus is Lord over those who have wronged you. If they are believers, pray that He will work in their hearts and bring them to repentance, which is essential for restoring their broken relationship with you. And as you pray, remember that they have become ensnared by the "Devil's trap, having been captured to do his will" (2 Timothy 2:26b, HCSB). They have allowed Satan to influence them for ungodly purposes and are accountable for their actions.

If those who wronged you are not believers, pray for their salvation and follow the example of our patient and loving God, who does not want "anyone to perish, but everyone to come to repentance" (2 Peter 3:9b). Remember that your testimony and their salvation are more important than your personal vindication, reputation or comfort. Jesus is Lord over all, including those who neither know nor care about Him.

Submit from the Heart

American culture doesn't value submission. For many people, it's a sign of weakness, inferiority or failure. Success and significance, they believe, comes through strength, superiority and achievement.

A similar mindset prevailed in New Testament times. The mighty Roman Empire was built on sheer military power, bringing the *Pax Romana* ("the Roman peace") to the world as its legions conquered or intimidated nation after nation. In Roman society, submission was reserved for vanquished peoples, women, children, and slaves – those who were weak, powerless and disenfranchised. Jewish society had a similar way of viewing submissiveness.

Against this cultural backdrop James wrote, "Submit yourselves, then, to God....Humble yourselves before the Lord, and he will lift you up" (James 4:7a,10). These commands required a radically new perspective for those who sought to live a life pleasing to God. They're equally radical and applicable to us today.

Salvation Begins with Submission

Salvation requires a submissive, tender and broken heart. Remember that God "saved us, not because of righteous things we had done, but because of his mercy. He saved us through the washing of rebirth and renewal by the Holy Spirit, whom he poured out on us generously through Jesus Christ our Savior" (Titus 3:5-6). We are grateful recipients of a salvation we did not earn or deserve. Even the faith to believe the gospel was God's gracious and precious gift to us (Ephesians 2:8-9). Because God loved us when we were unlovable and drew us to Himself through the convicting power of the Holy Spirit, we saw ourselves as God viewed us – as sinners in need of God's grace. Turning from our sin (repentance), we believed that Christ died on the cross to pay the penalty we deserved to pay. By faith, we received Christ as Lord and began living in newness of life (Ephesians 4:22-24).

Submission to God was repulsive and impossible prior to our salvation. Now that we are "a new creation" in

Christ, "new things have come" (2 Corinthians 5:17, HCSB), including the desire to submit to God's will for our lives. Submission to God is now a joyful, daily experience. We desire to submit to Him because we love Him and know that He wants what is best for us.

Following Jesus' Example

Although Jesus was "in the beginning...with God" and "all things were created through Him" (John 1:1-3), Jesus submitted Himself to the authority of His earthly parents (Luke 2:51) and His heavenly Father (John 8:42; 10:37-38; 17:1-12). He humbled himself and served His disciples in many ways, most strikingly when He washed their feet (John 13:1-17). In the Garden of Gethsemane Jesus prayed, "Father...not My will, but Yours, be done" (Luke 22:42, HCSB). Soon afterward, He was "obedient unto death" on the cross, bringing salvation to all who believe (Philippians 2:8-11).

We are called to follow Jesus' example. We should want to follow His example of submitting to God and one another. "Make your own attitude that of Christ Jesus" (Philippians 2:5, HCSB) and "Submit to one another out of reverence for Christ" (Ephesians 5:21) are not optional suggestions for the fully devoted follower of Christ; they are commands that we should obey willingly and joyously.

Ben chafed under the leadership of the new deacon chairman. Ben knew that Rob had wanted to be chairman of the deacons for many years, apparently for the wrong reasons. Rob was the president or leader of nearly everything that he was involved with, including his job. He was an aggressive "go-getter" who craved leadership and achievement. From Ben's perspective, becoming deacon chair appeared to be another accomplishment that Rob could add to his already lengthy resumé.

Ben had other reasons to be concerned about Rob's leadership. While Rob was a good guy, he didn't seem very spiritual. He was interested in church facilities and financial affairs, not mentoring men and building disciples. Ben knew that someone had to oversee the physical aspects of the church's ministry. However, he believed that the deacon chairman should be a spiritual man who was actively involved in the spiritual ministries of the congregation.

Ben weighed his options. He could voice his objections even though the deacon body had just elected Rob to be the chairman. He could serve as deacon begrudgingly and warily. Or he could submit to Rob's leadership and invite Rob to become involved in a men's weekly discipleship group.

The choice for Ben was clear. Submission wasn't easy but it was the only way that Ben could honor God with his attitude and actions. Ben prayed, "Father, not my will, but yours, be done." Ben could pray for Rob daily and ask God to change Rob's heart and priorities.

Biblical Submission and Authority

In Romans 13:1, the verb "be subject" (KJV) or "submit" (NIV) is translated from the Greek word *hupotasso*. It is a military term that means "to arrange (troop divisions) in a military fashion under the command of a leader."[37] *Hupotasso* involves placing "ourselves under submission to authorities with the full intent of obeying them."[38] As Ben discovered in the incident just described, it's not always easy to submit to the authority of others, especially when we question their spiritual qualifications or integrity.

John Bevere describes two kinds of biblical authority in his book Under Cover. God's direct authority in our lives involves submitting to the teaching of His written Word and the guidance of His Spirit. God's indirect or delegated authority is expressed in four distinct ways. Bevere writes, "The New Testament speaks of four divisions of delegated authority: civil, church, family, and social."[39] These areas are described in the following biblical passages:

- Civil (Romans 13:1-3; 1 Timothy 2:1-2; Titus 3:1; 1 Peter 2:13-14)

- Church (Ephesians 5:21; 1 Peter 5:5-6; Hebrews 13:17; 1 Peter 5:1-3)

- Family (Colossians 3:18-19; Ephesians 5:22-28; 1 Peter 3:1-7; Ephesians 6:1-3; Colossians 3:20-21)

- Social (1 Peter 2:18-24; Ephesians 6:5-9)

There's a strong link between God's direct and delegated authority. When we're submissive to God's direct authority in our lives, we'll also be submissive to His delegated authority in our government as well as in our churches, families and workplaces. Conversely, it's very likely that we're rebelling against God's Word and chafing under Christ's lordship when we harbor a rebellious spirit toward government officials, spiritual leaders, husbands/fathers, or employers.

Understanding Delegated Authority

God does not delegate His authority randomly. He has specific reasons for allowing people to assume positions of authority in the four areas described above. Sometimes God's reasons are understood quickly and are easy for us to accept. Other times we will not know until we get to heaven why God allowed certain individuals to exercise authority over our lives, especially when that authority is unjust and ungodly.

Unconditional Submission and Conditional Obedience

John Bevere insightfully observes that "obedience deals with our responsive actions toward authority. Submission deals with our attitude toward authority. This is where most of us miss it."[40]   God calls us to be completely submissive and obedient to His direct authority in our lives (His Word and Spirit). He also expects us to be completely submissive in our attitude toward His delegated authority in our government, workplaces, churches, and homes. However, because delegated authority is human and imperfect, our obedience to delegated authority is conditional. There are rare occasions when our obedience to Christ requires us to disobey sinful human authorities.

Our disobedience to delegated authority doesn't give us the right to avoid the consequences of our actions or be disrespectful toward those whom God has placed in authority over us. We must remain submissive to their leadership and respectful to their positions, graciously accepting the consequences of our disobedience and trusting God to intervene in the situation according to His wisdom and timing.

In Acts 5 the apostles were flogged for disobeying the Sanhedrin's order to stop preaching (Acts 5:40). Rather than resent what had happened to them, they maintained a respectful attitude toward the Sanhedrin, "rejoicing that they were counted worthy to be dishonored on behalf of the name [of Jesus]" (Acts 5:41, HCSB). On the other hand, the apostles continued to disobey the Sanhedrin's order: "Every day...they continued teaching and proclaiming the good news that the Messiah is Jesus" (Acts 5:42, HCSB).

The Bible contains several other examples of unconditional submission and conditional obedience:

- David and Saul (1 Samuel 24:1-7; 26:1-11)

- Shadrach, Meshach, Abednego, and King Nebuchadnezzar (Daniel 3)

- Daniel and King Darius (Daniel 6)

- Peter and John before the Sanhedrin (Acts 4:18,19,31)

- Paul before the high priest Ananias (Acts 23:1-5)

A Caution about Disobeying God's Delegated Authority

Most of the time we are not faced with situations that require disobedience toward God's delegated authority. We should be extremely careful to discern if God's purposes and Word are being violated by human authorities. Sometimes it is tempting for us to cloak our disobedience to authority with spiritual rationalizations. As John Bevere has noted,

> Ninety-nine percent of the problems that people have obeying is not when leaders tell them to sin but just telling them things they don't want to do. Submission does not mean "I submit as long as I agree." Submission doesn't even begin until there's disagreement. The only time we're not to obey is when we're told to do something contrary to the written Word of God.[41]

God Receives Glory from Our Submission and Obedience

When our attitudes are submissive toward God and to those whom He has given authority, "men will praise God for the obedience that accompanies your confession of the gospel of Christ" (2 Corinthians 9:13). Submission is all about our attitude toward God and what He has established – not about our agreement or disagreement.

He must receive the glory from everything we do, just as our Lord sought to glorify His heavenly Father in everything He did:

> Father...I have glorified You on the earth by completing the work You gave Me to do (John 17:1a,4, HCSB).

Consider praying right now and ask God to break through your unsubmissive heart and help you relinquish anything that keeps you from being obedient to His Word. Pray for those in authority over you. Ask God to show you ways that you can come under their authority and serve with glad and thankful hearts. If an authority figure is in direct conflict with God's Word, ask God to strengthen your resolve to be obedient to Him. Ask for wisdom and discernment so you don't spiritualize rebellion. Whatever course of action you choose, your heart and actions must glorify God.

Win the Enemy, Not the Fight

Angela could not understand how Liz and Jack could continue to be friendly toward her, much less speak to her. Five months earlier Angela had spread several vicious lies about them among the members of Covenant of Grace Church, claiming that Liz and Jack had treated her unfairly in a joint business venture. When their partnership hadn't taken the direction that Angela wanted, she left the business abruptly and smeared Liz and Jack's reputation in ways that no one could prove or disprove.

Angela was dumbfounded over Liz and Jack's response to her. Rather than take legal action against her for breaking her financial obligations and slandering them, Liz and Jack continued to reach out to her through notes in the mail and smiles at church. They didn't gloss over what Angela had done, but their actions clearly demonstrated their unconditional love for Angela.

Angela was unnerved and uncertain about how to relate to Liz and Jack. Rather than come to terms with the ways she had treated them, she began to avoid them. Angela knew that she had treated Liz and Jack horribly, yet they continued to love her.

God's love is a redeeming love. He reached out to us before we trusted Him. He loved us deeply, intentionally and tenaciously, seeking to redeem us from our sinful, self-destructive ways by giving us new life through His Son, Jesus Christ.

"To redeem" means to deliver something or someone by payment of a price. In the Old Testament a person would redeem or buy back property, animals and even people who had become legally obligated to a third party. People who had encountered financial problems and become indentured slaves could be freed when someone (often a relative known as a kinsman redeemer) would pay their debt.

Several Old Testament prophets and writers declared that Israel desperately needed redemption from its spiritual enslavement to sin. Through the prophet Hosea, God said, "Woe to them, because they have strayed from me! Destruction to them, because they have rebelled against me! I long to redeem them but they speak lies against me" (Hosea 7:13). The psalmist implored the Israelites to drawn close to God by writing, "O Israel, put your hope in the LORD, for with the LORD is unfailing love and with him is full redemption. He himself will redeem Israel from all their sins" (Psalm 130:7-8).

> God's love is a redeeming love. He loves us deeply, intentionally, and tenaciously.

The New Testament describes how Jesus Christ paid the ultimate price for our sin by dying on the cross. Peter writes, "For you know that you were redeemed from your empty way of life inherited from the fathers, not with perishable things, like silver or gold, but with the precious blood of Christ, like that of a lamb without defect or blemish" (1 Peter 1:18-19, HCSB). Because God loves us so much, he "bought us back" (redeemed us) from our enslaved condition by paying for our sin with the precious blood of His Son. This is love – redemptive love!

Liz and Jack understood the implications of these profound truths for their daily lives. They were no longer free to live according to their old, sinful ways (1 Corinthians 6:19-20). They didn't want to live like that any more. They were free from their sin, free to love God and free to love others with the love of God. That's why they could love Angela even though she had hurt them so deeply. Liz and Jack knew that God's redeeming love was deeper and greater than Angela's sinful actions. They knew that God could use them to demonstrate His redeeming love to Angela by loving her deeply, intentionally and tenaciously.

Love Deeply

> *Living above with saints we love*
> *that will be grace and glory;*
> *living below with saints we know*
> *that is a different story.*

Most of us have heard this old doggerel and smiled, but often there's more truth in it than we'd care to admit. Judging by the biblical record, as well our own experience, living life together as God's people is not easy. Yet God expects us to do more than merely coexist or endure one another. He calls us to "love one another deeply, from the heart" (1 Peter 1:22b). The word "deeply" also can be translated "fervently, earnestly, or intently," indicating that our love for one another in the Body of Christ must be a heartfelt, consuming commitment.

God loves us deeply. After Judah's sin brought the nation judgment, devastation and captivity in Babylon, God reaffirmed His deep, earnest love for His people by saying, "I have loved you with an everlasting love; therefore, I have continued to extend faithful love to you" (Jeremiah 31:3b, HCSB). Centuries later God demonstrated the full extent of His love on the cross of Jesus Christ: "For God so loved the world that he gave his one and only Son" (John 3:16b). Today God reaches out to us with that same deep, earnest love, and He calls us to follow His example in the way we love one another.

Loving other believers deeply from the heart prepares us for resolving church conflict by enabling us to look beyond offenses and see the spiritual needs of others. As the Apostle Peter wrote, "Above all, love each other deeply, because love covers over a multitude of sins" (1 Peter 4:8). The strength and depth of our love for other Christians prior to a difficulty determines our ability to love them redemptively and offer forgiveness during and after a conflict.

Love Intentionally

Jesus turned the world's wisdom upside down when he taught us to "love your enemies, do good to those who hate you, bless those who curse you, pray for those who mistreat you" (Luke 6:27-28, HCSB). This is not our natural response when others hurt us. If we react to wrongdoing according to our sinful nature, we will perpetuate a vicious, downward cycle of conflict. However, as Christians we can choose to allow God's supernatural grace and presence to fill our lives and stop this cycle before it spirals out of control. We can choose in faith to be filled with God's Spirit and respond to wrongdoing redemptively and intentionally.

The Apostle Paul describes intentional love in Romans 12:17-21:

> Do not repay anyone evil for evil. Be careful to do what is right in the eyes of everybody. If it is possible, as far as it depends on you, live at peace with everyone. Do not take revenge, my friends, but leave room for God's wrath, for it is written: "It is mine to avenge; I will repay," says the Lord. On the contrary: "If your enemy is hungry, feed him; if he is thirsty, give him something to drink. In doing this, you will heap burning coals on his head." Do not be overcome by evil, but overcome evil with good.

Loving intentionally means that we avoid reacting in kind to sinful words and actions. Rather than be overcome by the sinful ways of hurtful people, we choose to offer them God's grace and love. This provides an opportunity for God to work in their lives and convict them of their sinful ways.

John MacArthur has commented on Romans 12:21 by writing,

> We must not allow the evil done to us by other people to overcome and overwhelm us. Second, and even more important, we must not allow ourselves to be overcome by our own evil responses. Our own evil is infinitely more detrimental to us than is the evil done to us by others.[42]

Love Tenaciously

Numerous passages throughout the Old Testament refer to God's "steadfast love" or *hesed*. This Hebrew word can be translated as mercy, kindness, love, or loyalty, depending on its context. God's steadfast love is not a "virtue or personality trait" but something He does as He relates to His people.[43] God's love is not a passing emotion but an unfaltering expression of His covenant faithfulness to His people. There is nothing that we can do that will cause Him to love us more or less. God's steadfast love is a loyal, faithful love that seeks what is best for us.

In the Old Testament, God called the Israelites to have relationships characterized by *hesed* when he commanded them "to act justly and to love mercy" (Micah 6:8). In the New Testament, God's tenacious love is expressed by the Greek word *agape*. Like *hesed*, *agape* love is unconditional and sacrificial. As the Apostle Paul wrote in Romans 5:8, "God proves His own [*agape*] love for us in that while we were still sinners Christ died for us!" (HCSB)

We show God's *agape* love to other people when we love them unconditionally and sacrificially. This kind of love motivates and directs our use of spiritual gifts in the church (1 Corinthians 13) and describes how we should love other believers (John 15:12), our neighbors (Matthew 5:43) and even our enemies (Matthew 5:44).

> We love because he
> first loved us.
> *1 John 4:19*

Seek Wisdom from Above

Gene vainly attempted to hold back his anger over the way a family at Open Arms Fellowship treated his neighbors who were attending worship for the first time. Like other first-time guests, the couple assumed they could sit in any empty pew in the sanctuary. They had just found a spot about a third of the way from the back when the church family who usually sat there gruffly asked them to move from "their pew." The couple quickly moved to the other side of the sanctuary, confused and hurt over this rude and unexpected welcome.

Gene couldn't focus on God during the worship service as he mulled over the incident. All he could think about was confronting that family the moment the service was finished. How uncaring and audacious! Gene's anger was fueled by the fact that he had spent almost a year inviting his young neighbors to church. Now, all of his effort and prayer seemed to be destroyed in one thoughtless moment.

Gene walked over to the church family immediately after the benediction. He was more than ready to unload everything he was feeling. Then he remembered Proverbs 29:11 - "A fool gives full vent to his anger; but a wise man keeps himself under control."

The Way of Wisdom

We desperately need God's wisdom when emotions run high and tempers flare. Left to our own ways, we tend to react defensively and sometimes aggressively to difficult situations rather than respond biblically through the power of God's Spirit. We need God's wisdom to act lovingly and redemptively in conflicted situations.

Wisdom is more than merely knowing the truth; we possess wisdom as we apply the truth of God's Word to our everyday lives. We live wisely as we trust God's Word over our feelings and perceptions, choosing in faith to obey how He has told us to live. Moses expressed this principle long ago when he told the Israelites,

> See, I have taught you decrees and laws as the LORD my God commanded me, so that you may follow them in the land you are entering to take possession of it. Observe them carefully, for this will show your wisdom and understanding to the nations, who will hear about all these decrees and say, "Surely this great nation is a wise and understanding people" (Deuteronomy 4:5-6).

The Beginning of Wisdom

Wisdom begins as we see ourselves and all of our human strengths, knowledge and resources in light of God's glorious majesty, infinite power and unsearchable wisdom. We possess true understanding as we shed the blindness of our myopic, self-centered ways and open ourselves to see God's person and character.

Most of us are familiar with the biblical story of Job's trials and suffering. He lost his family, possessions and health, as well as the respect of others. He struggled to understand why these calamities had befallen him, sometimes approaching God with an accusing and complaining spirit (Job 23:1-4). Yet when God revealed His glory to Job, Job's outlook changed dramatically.[44] His immediate circumstances hadn't changed but his heart and perspective were transformed. Job humbled himself before God and said,

> Surely I spoke about things I did not understand, things too wonderful for me to know....I had heard rumors about You [God], but now my eyes have seen You. Therefore I take back my words and repent in dust and ashes (Job 42:3b,5-6, HCSB).

Once the condition of Job's heart was right, God made everything else right in his life, restoring Job's temporal blessings: "The LORD blessed the latter part of Job's life more than the first" (Job 42:12).

Job discovered what the Bible calls the "fear of the LORD." When we begin to experience God personally and biblically, our lives are radically reoriented. Then we can grasp the truth of Proverbs 9:10: "The fear of the LORD is the beginning of wisdom, and knowledge of the Holy One is understanding." The "fear of the LORD" comes as we have a profound and submissive reverence for God. We consciously cease to be the center of our lives, choosing instead to give God His rightful place in everything we are and do.

People who seek after wisdom that is void of God seek in vain. The Book of Proverbs calls them "fools," not because they are intellectually deficient but because they refuse to place God at the center of their lives. In light of eternity and the many negative consequences they will experience in life, their decision to reject God is truly foolish. "The fool says in his heart, 'God does not exist'" (Psalm 14:1; 53:1, HCSB).

Discovering God's Wisdom in the Midst of Conflict

Our best preparation for addressing conflict biblically and constructively arises out of our daily relationship with God. If we place Him at the center of our lives, seek to apply the wisdom of His Word in our lives, submit to Christ's lordship and allow God's Spirit to fill us, we'll be prepared to respond to conflict. For the Christian, conflict resolution is not a management technique or easy three-step process that can be used to manipulate others for selfish purposes. Conflict resolution is a lifestyle that originates out of our peace with God and flows naturally into our relationships with other people.

Believers who are committed to knowing and obeying God's Word will discover a treasure trove of wisdom in the Bible for personal conflict resolution and peacemaking. We've had opportunity to learn how helpful and practical God's Word is in these areas in the previous chapters of this book. James makes a clear connection between practical, godly wisdom, spiritual warfare, the fruit of heavenly wisdom in our lives, and biblical peacemaking:

Who is wise and understanding among you? Let him show it by his good life, by deeds done in the humility that comes from wisdom. But if you harbor bitter envy and selfish ambition in your hearts, do not boast about it or deny the truth. Such "wisdom" does not come down from heaven but is earthly, unspiritual, of the devil. For where you have envy and selfish ambition, there you find disorder and every evil practice.

But the wisdom that comes from heaven is first of all pure; then peace-loving, considerate, submissive, full of mercy and good fruit, impartial and sincere. Peacemakers who sow in peace raise a harvest of righteousness (James 3:13-18).

Trust God

There are many ways that we seek to justify our failure to trust God during troubled times:

- We're angry – we believe we have the right to be upset

- We've been hurt deeply – we're not ready to forgive

- We're impatient – God's timetable is exasperating!

- We're afraid – we feel vulnerable

- We're confused – God's apparent plan isn't making sense

- We're lonely – God seems to have deserted us

- We're stubborn – we want to resolve conflict our own way

The list of excuses and rationalizations is almost endless! When we refuse to trust God during times of conflict, we substitute His presence and blessing for a variety of self-centered and miserable experiences. Too often we resist surrendering to the lordship of Jesus Christ, even though we continue to hurt ourselves, other believers and our churches.

Trusting God During Troubled Times

King David certainly experienced many difficulties and conflicts in his lifetime. As a boy David faced attacks by wild animals, the ridicule of his brothers and the giant warrior Goliath. Later David spent years fleeing from Saul's relentless, murderous pursuit. Even after being firmly established as king of Israel, David faced the heartbreaking rebellion of his son Absalom as well as several other occasions when enemies threatened the security of Israel.

Rather than blame God or others for his circumstances, David trusted God completely, confident that God and God alone was his strength and refuge. Psalm 62:5-8 reveals David's heart as he expresses his absolute reliance on God:

> Find rest, O my soul, in God alone; my hope comes from him. He alone is my rock and my salvation; he is my fortress, I will not be shaken. My salvation and my honor depend on God; he is my mighty rock, my refuge. Trust in him at all times, O people; pour out your hearts to him, for God is our refuge.

King David could trust God because he understood God's character and ways. David knew from personal experience how God is wonderfully omniscient (Psalm 139), magnificently omnipotent (Psalm 136), absolutely good (Psalm 34:8), infinitely loving (Psalm 100:5), and amazingly forgiving (Psalm 51). For David, God was not an abstract, disinterested "higher power" but a loving shepherd who was intimately involved in David's daily life – caring, renewing, guiding, and protecting him (Psalm 23:1-4).

Trusting God in the midst of church conflict is not easy but is essential for allowing God to work in the situation. Trust involves choosing to base our attitudes and actions on God's nature, character and promises – not our emotions or current circumstances. We can trust God to lead us through troubled times because He knows every aspect of the conflict, including the hearts of those who struggle against us. We can be confident in God's power to work for our good in all circumstances, even when the outlook appears to be bleak.

> And we know that in all things God works for the good of those who love him, who have been called according to his purpose.
> *Romans 8:28*

Jared was called to serve as the pastor of Victory Valley Church four years ago. Initially there was an air of excitement among church members as baptisms, attendance, and giving increased dramatically. Nearly everyone sensed that God was working powerfully in the congregation.

Then a women's class began to be dissatisfied with Jared's leadership. They disliked the new worship music, felt threatened by the people who were joining the church, and questioned Jared's time management and priorities. A few of the ladies complained that Jared was neglecting them and other longtime members. Gradually some of the women's husbands adopted their wives' critical spirit and began to speak openly about Jared's resignation.

Jared wondered how these church members could be so negative when God was working in the church in such powerful and obvious ways. It wasn't easy to endure their criticism, but Jared clung to God's promises, confident in his calling to serve as pastor of the congregation.

Trusting Is Obeying

We trust God when we acknowledge the truthfulness of what He has said through our faithful obedience. "Doers" and not "hearers" of God's Word are those who genuinely trust God. As James writes, "Do not merely listen to the word, and so deceive yourselves. Do what it says" (James 1:22). Trusting God is not an emotion but an act of the will which results in faithful obedience. We trust God when we acknowledge the truthfulness of His Word and put it into practice, believe that His methods are the best methods of resolving conflict and wait patiently for Him to act in our circumstances.

Trusting God's Truth

The only real truth is God's truth, especially when controversy and confusion erupt in church. The Bible illuminates hearts that are darkened by sin, teaches us how to relate to one another in the Body of Christ and provides practical instruction on forgiveness and reconciliation. As the storms of conflict swirl around us, only God's Word offers us the truth on which to anchor our lives.

Unfortunately, far too often we rush to resolve church conflict without prayerfully seeking what God has told us in the Bible. No wonder so many conflicts blaze into uncontrollable firestorms! Only God's Word sanctifies our attitudes and actions, enabling us to examine our hearts and motives and respond to conflict in godly ways.

Trusting God's Methods

Let's face it! Biblical conflict resolution is completely unconventional and even foolish by the world's standards. Biblical conflict resolution begins with examining ourselves to determine if we need to remove the "log" from our own eyes (Matthew 7:3-5). Worldly conflict resolution uses principles of negotiation which seek to achieve the best possible outcome for each person involved in the conflict. Biblical conflict resolution requires us to relinquish our rights for the good of others and the glory of God.

Trusting God's Timing

Sometimes conflict can be resolved quickly and easily, especially when it involves a minor disagreement or misunderstanding or has not escalated into a churchwide controversy. Many times, however, conflict is not resolved quickly or privately and seems to drag on endlessly. We cry out for immediate relief from the pain of conflict. God wants us to trust Him. After we have done everything that His Word instructs us to do, He wants us to wait on Him and His timing so that we can see Him at work and give Him the glory when authentic reconciliation occurs.

Trusting God means that we will let God be God and not vainly attempt to usurp His rightful role in our lives and in our congregations. God views our conflicts from the standpoint of eternity, and He knows when our hearts are truly ready for reconciliation. The Lord is never slow to act on our behalf. His timing is impeccable. In fact, God's timing is perfect!

When We Trust God

Trusting God fuels our faith. We lay down our own understanding and rely on God's sovereignty. When we trust God, we allow Him the room in our lives to prove Himself to us. In Malachi 3:6-10, God asks His people to trust His provision. His requirement of the tithe was a way to stretch their faith. They had to relinquish in order to receive. His promise to them is no less amazing to us today. Like the words of the old hymn, "Trust me, try Me, prove Me, sayeth the Lord of Host," God speaks a blessing in His challenge. "Test me in this," says the Lord Almighty, "and see if I will not throw open the floodgates of heaven and pour out so much blessing that you will not have room enough for it" (Malachi 3:10). WOW! Who couldn't take that kind of blessing? That's worth a little bit of trust!

When we trust God, we cannot be shaken (Psalm 125:1); God becomes our strength, our joy and our song (Isaiah 12:2); and we give Him the opportunity to be God – God Almighty, God the Most High – in our lives. When we trust God, He acts and we can rest! We can have more than a trouble–free mind; we can have perfect peace. "You will keep in perfect peace him whose mind is steadfast, because he trusts in you" (Isaiah 26:3).

In times of conflict, we can trust God's truth, God's methods and God's timing. We can trust because He is perfect!

The Ways of a Peacemaker

The Prince of Peace has high expectations for His followers, and those who would be His disciples are called to walk on a higher road. We are to keep our hearts and minds focused on our Lord and Savior, even as the fires of conflict rage around us. We have the privilege and joy of walking in the Spirit and bearing the fruit of a Spirit-filled life in all situations, including church conflict. This supernatural endowment gives us the ability to "speak the truth in love" as we glorify God with our lives and in our churches.

This chapter teaches us how to live according to the ways of a peacemaker and challenges us to remain steadfast in our commitments to Christ and His Church.

Glorify God

Soli Deo Gloria - "glory to God alone." This great cry of the Reformation has inspired and challenged Christians through the centuries. It declares that everything we are and do as believers must glorify God. As the majestic Sovereign of the universe, God alone deserves our honor, praise and obedience.

God is worthy of our adoration when life is going well and when it goes awry. He has not changed when conflict engulfs our congregations. We are the ones who have sinned and fallen short of God's glory (Romans 3:23). While Satan tempts us to react to conflict sinfully and worsen the problems in our churches, God's Word calls us to glorify Him through the ways we respond to conflict.

> So whether you eat or drink or whatever you do, do it all for the glory of God.
> *1 Corinthians 10:31*

The peacemaker understands that we must look to God, depend on Him and seek to glorify His name when conflict arises. The peacemaker knows that God's redeeming power can transform conflict to victory. He recognizes that when conflict comes, his role is to lift God's name above the fray so others will see God's glory. Finally, the peacemaker knows that even conflict is an opportunity to reflect God's nature through his own attitudes and actions. There is no fear in conflict, only resolute determination to exalt God's glory – *Soli Deo Gloria*!

Glimpsing God's Glory

God's glory almost defies explanation because of His absolute splendor, holiness and magnificence. Our human limitations prevent us from completely understanding His glory. Like Moses, we would literally die if we were directly exposed to God's awesome presence (Exodus 33:20). Consequently, God has chosen to reveal himself in ways that we can glimpse but never fully grasp this side of heaven.

Psalm 19:1 tells us that "the heavens declare the glory of God." This verse tells us that the grandeur of creation offers meaningful insight into "God's invisible qualities – his eternal power and divine nature" (Romans 1:20a). God's self-disclosure through wonders of the universe is so "plain" or evident that we're "without excuse" if we deny His existence and fail to glorify Him as God (Romans 1:19-21).

God's glory is the way He deliberately and lovingly shows us His nature, character and attributes. When God reveals His glory to us, we discover what He wants us to know about Him. For example, when God's glory passed by Moses on Mount Sinai, He revealed important aspects of His nature that the Israelites desperately needed to know.

> Then the Lord came down in a cloud and stood there with him; and he called out his own name, Yahweh. The LORD passed in front of Moses, calling out, "Yahweh! The LORD! The God of compassion and mercy! I am slow to anger and filled with unfailing love and faithfulness. I lavish unfailing love to a thousand generations. I forgive iniquity, rebellion, and sin. But I do not excuse the guilty. I lay the sins of the parents upon their children and grandchildren; the entire family is affected – even children in the third and fourth generations" (Exodus 34:5-7, NLT).

God wanted Moses to focus on His redeeming nature rather than His appearance. Following the Israelites' gross disobedience and idolatry with the golden calf (Exodus 32-34), God desired to renew the people's relationship to Him with a covenant (Exodus 34:10). God wanted the Israelites to know that He would deal with them fairly and compassionately, forgiving their sin and loving them. That is why God described His nature and character (His glory) to Moses as He passed by Moses on the mountainside. God revealed that He is compassionate, merciful, slow to anger, filled with unfailing love, faithful, and just. God wanted Moses to behold His glory and understand who He was in relation to the spiritual needs of His people.

Take a few moments to consider the ways that you can be a peacemaker in your church and intentionally reflect the attributes of God listed in the Exodus passage:

- Compassionate   • Merciful

- Slow to anger   • Loving

- Faithful   • Just

Which one of these attributes is easiest for you to display in times of conflict? Which attribute is most difficult to display in times of conflict?

After Moses experienced God's glory, he "bowed to the ground at once and worshiped" (Exodus 34:8). Worship always has been a natural and necessary response to God's glory. When we get to know God better, we can't help but praise Him for His steadfast, unfailing love.

God's glory was expressed supremely through the incarnation of His Son, Jesus Christ: "The Word became flesh and made his dwelling among us. We have seen his glory, the glory of the One and Only, who came from the Father, full of grace and truth" (John 1:14). Once again, God's self-revealing glory disclosed something significant about His nature. Through Christ's life, death and resurrection, God displayed the fullness of His "grace and truth."

On one occasion Jesus declared unequivocally, "Anyone who has seen me has seen the Father" (John 14:9). Jesus enabled the glory of God to be seen through His absolute obedience to the Father's will (Luke 22:42). As Jesus prayed before His crucifixion, "Father, the time has come. Glorify your Son, that your Son may glorify you. I have brought you glory on earth by completing the work you gave me to do. I have revealed you to those whom you gave me out of the world" (John 17:1b,4,6a).

The greatest conflict on earth surrounded the arrest, trial, crucifixion, and death of Christ. Yet Christ was not victimized by the conflict. By doing God's will He was the glorious victor in every step on the road to Calvary. As peacemakers we can experience victory by having the mind of Christ and displaying God's attributes, His glory, in the midst of conflict.

The Weight of Glory

The Hebrew word for glory is *kabod*. It refers to the heavy, weighty presence of God. We cannot experience God's glory and remain unaffected. His glory is unforgettable, leaving a profound impression on us as we encounter Him.

As we've just read in the Book of Exodus, Moses fell down in worship after experiencing God's glory on Mount Sinai (Exodus 34:8). When construction of the tabernacle was complete, Moses could not enter it because of the intensity of God's glory (Exodus 40:35). Likewise, when Solomon dedicated the temple with a magnificent praise and worship service, the priests were forced to leave the temple because "the glory of the LORD filled the temple of God" (2 Chronicles 5:13-14).

The Holy of Holies, the inner sanctuary of the tabernacle and later the temple, contained the Ark of the Covenant. Once a year, the high priest entered the Holy Place to make atonement for the sins of the people. God certainly considered His residence to be holy. If the high priest desecrated the Holy Place by not following God's precise instructions, he would die (Leviticus 16:2). God's holiness, His glory, is not a trifling matter.

> Woe is me, for I am ruined, because I am a man of unclean lips and live among a people of unclean lips, and because my eyes have seen the King, the LORD of Hosts.
> *Isaiah 6:5, HCSB*

The prophet Isaiah was completely undone when he saw a vision of God's glory (Isaiah 6:5). In the New Testament, the Apostle John fell in fear "like a dead man" after beholding the awesome glory of the resurrected Lord

(Revelation 1:17, HCSB). The peacemaker never loses this sense of awe as he or she beholds God's glory in His Word and in every circumstance of life, including church conflict.

Church controversy swirled all around Ida May, a church member well into her eighties. However, she joyfully stood firm on the Solid Rock of her life. She reminded everyone of a lighthouse in the midst of a storm. Waves of gossip, dissension, discord, and anger smashed against her, but she remained unmovable. Before the controversy, everyone in the church considered her their personal and favorite grandmother. Neither perceptions nor affections from any quarter changed her during the conflict.

Always faithful to her Lord, ever a beautiful reflection of God's glory in her own life, Ida May could not be shaken. Several times women she had known for years tried to pressure and coerce her to take sides. Her loyalties were with her Lord and she simply lifted both factions before God's throne. She exhibited compassion, a gentle tongue, and unconditional love for her brothers and sisters in Christ. Ida May was a peacemaker. She maintained the peace that Christ brought to her own heart. She refused to enter into the divisiveness of those who were determined to disrupt the church. God's glory had a life-changing effect on Ida May. As she reflected God's glory in the midst of conflict, others were changed by her testimony.

Reflecting the Lord's Glory

Today God's glory is present in people who are fully devoted followers of Jesus Christ. The temple in Jerusalem no longer exists; "We are the temple of the living God" (2 Corinthians 6:16). We experience God's glory as Christ dwells in us through the power of His Spirit. Just as Old Testament saints could not remain unaffected when they encountered God's glory, we too are changed by the glorious presence of Jesus in our lives:

And we, who with unveiled faces all reflect the Lord's glory, are being transformed into his likeness with ever-increasing glory, which comes from the Lord, who is the Spirit (2 Corinthians 3:18).

As we increasingly reflect the Lord's glory in our everyday lives, other people will come to know God better by watching Christ fill and transform our lives. Glorifying God is more than our personal devotion and commitment; it is allowing God's nature, character and attributes to flow through us to others.

Glorifying God in Church Conflict

How does experiencing God's glory through Jesus Christ prepare us to glorify God when conflict erupts in our churches?

First, because God's glory has enabled us to experience His mercy and forgiveness through Christ, we can be merciful and forgive others: "Bear with each other and forgive whatever grievances you may have against one another. Forgive as the Lord forgave you" (Colossians 3:13).

Second, because the glory of God's holiness and justice has enabled us to deal honestly with our sin, we can be humble and gracious in difficult situations, "speaking the truth in love" (Ephesians 4:15).

Third, because God's glory has shown us the unity that He has with His Son, we can maintain our unity in Christ despite the issues that threaten to tear us apart: "[I, Jesus, pray] that all of them may be one, Father, just as you are in me and I am in you. May they also be in us so that the world may believe that you have sent me. I have given them the glory that you gave me, that they may be one as we are one" (John 17:21-22).

Fourth, because God's glory was in the Light of the World, we can reflect Christ's light, His very countenance, when facing conflict. "For God, who said, 'Let light shine out of darkness,' made his light shine in our hearts to give us the light of the knowledge of the glory of God in the face of Christ" (2 Corinthians 4:6).

Finally, because God's glory reveals His sovereignty, power and majesty, we can trust His control over any church conflict, relinquishing our agenda and believing that God's plans and purposes will prevail. We can let go and focus on magnifying His name: "I will meditate on your wonderful works. They will tell of the power of your awesome works, and I will proclaim your great deeds" (Psalm 145:5b-6).

Focus on Christ

Cataracts of the Soul

It's exciting to be around new believers. For the first time in their lives they're experiencing the delight and wonder of being a "new creation" in Christ. Unlike many people who have attended church for years, "baby Christians" generally can't wait until their next opportunity to worship and pray with other believers, read their Bibles and share their faith. All things literally have become new for them, and it is exhilarating!

Unfortunately, the joy of new believers tends to diminish over time. Too many of them settle for spiritual mediocrity and immaturity. Churches frequently fail to help them to deepen their relationship with the Lord. Too many new believers lose their passion for knowing and serving Christ, joining the ranks of other church members who have serious but undiagnosed "spiritual cataracts."

Cataracts of the eye develop slowly over time as the lens of the eye ages and hardens, causing a person's vision to become increasingly cloudy and hazy. Most people who have their cataracts removed marvel over how clearly they can see. They knew they had vision problems prior to the cataract surgery, but they didn't know how truly impaired their vision had become until their cataracts were removed.

Take this "vision test" to check the condition of your spiritual eyes:

- Do you find it easier to see someone else's shortcomings before you see your own? (Luke 6:41-42)

- Do you look to your own interests rather than the interests of others? (Philippians 2:4)

- Do you focus more on the conflict and what people are doing rather than focusing on Jesus? (Hebrews 12:1-3)

- Do you look more at obstacles during tough times than at God's power to redeem a situation? (Numbers 13:32-33)

- Do you easily forget what your eyes have seen when God has worked things out in the past? (Deuteronomy 4:9-10)

The Bible instructs us to "examine yourselves to see whether you are in the faith; test yourselves. Do you not realize that Christ Jesus is in you – unless, of course, you fail the test?" (2 Corinthians 13:5)

How did you do on the spiritual vision test? If Christ is the Lord and focus of your life, your eyes will not develop spiritual cataracts. Hopefully, you answered "no" to all of the questions in the "vision test."

Cataracts of the soul are more debilitating to our well-being than cataracts of the eye since they prevent us from focusing on Christ. Spiritual cataracts are those attitudes and actions which gradually rob us of the joy of our salvation, our blessings in Christ and our commitment to follow Christ wholeheartedly. This dangerous spiritual condition directs the focus of our lives away from Christ and toward ourselves, causing us to disregard Christ's call to be His fully devoted followers: "If any of you wants to be my follower, you must turn from your selfish ways, take up your cross daily, and follow me" (Luke 9:23, NLT).

Spiritual blindness prevents us from resolving church conflict in ways that glorify God and build up the Body of Christ. Having lost our ability to see conflict from God's perspective, we, like Jesus' disciples, have "eyes but fail to see" (Mark 8:18). We've lost our ability to respond to conflict spiritually since we've lost our focus on Christ.

Stan had been a deacon at Legacy Park Church for nearly twenty years, attending worship services and church activities faithfully. He rarely missed the monthly deacon's meeting. Stan enjoyed going to church and valued the friendships that he had developed with many church members, but his relationship with the Lord had grown cold with the passage of time. Years had passed since Stan had read his Bible and prayed on a daily basis. Even more time had elapsed since he had shared his faith with another person. Church was a significant part of Stan's life, but somehow his relationship with Christ had become less important to him than when he had first placed his faith in Christ.

When an unexpected conflict erupted in Stan's church, he didn't know how to react. Stan wanted to help his pastor resolve the problem, but he didn't know what to do. He didn't even know how to pray.

Stan did the only thing he could do. He simply watched the conflict engulf the church, feeling powerless and useless as a deacon.

One day Stan opened his Bible, hoping that he would find a verse that would help his church. What he found changed his life dramatically. Stan fell to his knees weeping as he read Jesus' words in John 15:5. Even though he had heard them before, their truth pierced his heart as if he were reading them for the first time: "I am the vine; you are the branches. If a man remains in me and I in him, he will bear much fruit; apart from me you can do nothing."

A Passion for Knowing and Serving Christ

The Apostle Paul was incredibly passionate about following Jesus Christ. Nothing else mattered to him. Absolutely nothing. Paul considered everything that he had valued prior to becoming a Christian a total loss – mere rubbish. He wrote that nothing "compared to the surpassing greatness of knowing Christ Jesus my Lord;" nothing surpassed his longing "to know Christ and the power of his resurrection and the fellowship of sharing in his sufferings" (Philippians 3:10). Although Paul was near the end of his life when he penned these words, nothing had taken his focus off Christ. As a matter of fact, Paul's passion for the Lord had increased over the years.

What about your relationship with Christ? Has the focus of your life become blurred with the passage of time? Has your spiritual life been influenced by Paul's example – who was "off and running and…not turning back" to the very end of his life? As the following scripture passage indicates, total commitment is the only way we will reach the goal that God has set for our lives. Total commitment to Christ right now is the only way to prevent cataracts of the soul from developing in the future!

> I've got my eye on the goal, where God is beckoning us onward – to Jesus. I'm off and running, and I'm not turning back. So let's keep focused on that goal, those of us who want everything God has for us. If any of you have

something else in mind, something less than total commitment, God will clear your blurred vision – you'll see it yet! Now that we're on the right track, let's stay on it (Philippians 3:14-16, *The Message*).

An Ounce of Prevention Is Worth a Pound of Cure!

What draws you away from focusing your life on following Christ? As mentioned in the first chapter of this book, Satan has a wide variety of tactics that he uses against us, and each scheme is tailor-made for us!   Which of the following tend to blur your focus on Christ?

- Busy lifestyle   · Misplaced priorities

- Other people   · Worldly lures

- Kid's sports   · Little Bible knowledge

- Discouragement   · Weariness

- Something else?

As the old saying goes, "an ounce of prevention is worth a pound of cure." Most of us are aware of the temptations that Satan uses to draw us away from a close and growing relationship with Christ. We shouldn't despair if some of Satan's schemes seem to have been successful in the past. Understanding how Satan typically strikes us is the first step in avoiding his ploys in the future. Resolve today to "be strong in the Lord and in his mighty power. Put on the full armor of God so that you can take your stand against the devil's schemes....Stand firm then" (Ephesians 6:10,11,14a). The armor of God is a powerful preventative to Satan's wiles.

Focusing on Christ During Church Conflict

When Paul wrote to the problem-plagued Corinthian church, it's not surprising that he "resolved to know nothing while [he] was with [them] except Jesus Christ and him crucified" (1 Corinthians 2:2). He knew that the wisdom of God in Jesus Christ was far more powerful than human wisdom   (1 Corinthians 2:4). Nothing, not even a host of church problems, could take Paul's focus off Christ. We would be wise to follow his example when troubled times come to our congregations!

The fires of conflict raged almost uncontrollably at Quiet Meadows Church. Shepherding the church was not an easy task, and Pastor Dave was nearly overcome by nebulous complaints and unfounded accusations. He and other church members seemed to be constant targets. Weeks of conflict drained his energy and enthusiasm. It became a chore to go to the church office each day. Dave dreaded another barrage of criticism and "poison pen" letters. It was even more challenging to stand before the congregation each Sunday and preach.

He had to consciously curb his emotions, resisting reaction and the urge to publicly chastise the people who were destroying the Body of Christ. Dave wisely sought the godly counsel of one of his elders. Listening with deep understanding, the elder encouraged his pastor to continue preaching a new sermon series from the Gospel of John. "Stay focused on the cross," was the elder's sage advice. "When you direct our people to Jesus, He will take care of His beloved Bride. If you faithfully pastor the congregation and keep focused on Jesus," the elder said, "Christ will do the rest."

Dave followed the elder's advice in the ensuing months. It was amazing to see how God used the Gospel of John to address the needs of the congregation. Church members knew that Dave's messages came directly from the Bible as he preached verse-by-verse through John, week after week. Hearts were broken and healed by the power of God's Word.

Keep your eyes on Jesus, who both began and
finished this race we're in. Study how he did it.
Because he never lost sight of where he was
headed – that exhilarating finish in and with
God – he could put up with anything along the
way: cross, shame, whatever" (Hebrews 12:2,
The Message).

Speak the Truth in Love

*One Sunday after church, Pierce walked up to the new
couple who had been attending the church for only a few weeks.
He knew they were not believers yet, and wanted them to know
the truth about what they were getting into. Holding them
captive for nearly an hour, he launched off on the church and all
its problems.*
Identity: Pierce, The Piranha

*Weeping, Pansy stood up to leave the pastor's office. She had
shared her grief over the choices her friend was making. Pansy
had watched her friend commit adultery, wrecking her marriage
and the emotional stability of her children. But her pastor's
advice was unthinkable! How could she confront Sandra? She
didn't want to ruin their friendship.*
Identity: Pansy, The Pacifist

Speaking the truth in love, we will in all things
grow up into him who is the Head, that is,
Christ (Ephesians 4:15).

The Apostle Paul's love for the Bride of Christ
compelled him to cover her with God's truth. He
understood the only real way to express love for the
church was to preserve truth. Truth without love is harsh
and empty, nothing: "If I have the gift of prophecy [truth
telling] and can fathom all mysteries and all knowledge,

and if I have a faith that can move mountains, but have not love, I am nothing" (1 Corinthians 13:2). Truth and love are inseparable. Paul warns his young protégé, Timothy, to be on guard for false teachers who were trying to remove truth from the church. Paul instructed Timothy to take charge of the situation and to command the false teachers to quit teaching. He then insightfully adds that the basis of the command, the motive behind it, is love, "The goal of this command is love, which comes from a pure heart and a good conscience and a sincere faith" (1 Timothy 1:5). Paul kills two birds with one stone of instruction. Don't condone falsehood, but don't abandon love in the process.

Peter underscored this dynamic principle in 1 Peter 1:22 - "Now that you have purified yourselves by obeying the truth so that you have sincere love for your brothers, love one another deeply, from the heart." We purify ourselves and our churches with truth. God cleanses us with His truth so that we can love one another properly, with sincere, deep love from a transformed heart. If we separate truth from love, we distort what Christ has given us. We receive His truth and it roots us, establishes us and enables us to love as He loved.

The New Living Translation renders Ephesians 3:19 as, "May you experience the love of Christ, though it is too great to understand fully. Then you will be made complete with all the fullness of life and power that comes from God." We cannot conceive the expanse of Christ's love for us. It's too great! Yet, isn't it just like God to allow us to experience and to be empowered by something we can't fully understand? Christ's love fills us with God's incredible power, enabling us to know and speak His truth.

However, we see many different responses in how church members relate to truth and one another as conflict escalates. Some prefer to avoid conflict at all costs, literally. Others seem to relish conflict. Not only do they enter a fray, they are not beyond starting it. They have a strong opinion about the situation, and will speak it regardless of the damage that ensues. All too rarely, there are the precious peacemakers who understand the biblical principle of speaking the truth in love.

The Message paraphrases Paul's instruction in 1 Timothy 1:5 that we examined earlier: "The whole point of what we're urging is simply love – love uncontaminated by self-interest and counterfeit faith, a life open to God. Those who fail to keep to this point soon wander off into cul-de-sacs of gossip. They set themselves up as experts on religious issues, but haven't the remotest idea of what they're holding forth with such imposing eloquence."

> And I pray that you, being rooted and established in love, may have power, together with all the saints, to grasp how wide and long and high and deep is the love of Christ, and to know this love that surpasses knowledge – that you may be filled to the measure of all the fullness of God.
> *Ephesians 3:17b-19*

"Cul-de-sacs" of gossip. That's the street you wander down when you veer either direction from full truth or complete love. Judgment without truth makes one an imposter. Truth without love is empty. Love without truth is vain. All are dead-end streets. One must know the truth, possess Christ's love, then speak the truth in love.

The way a person responds to conflict provides a window to his or her heart and falls into four basic categories. We will examine four general ways people respond to conflict, how they handle the truth and whether or not they extend Christ's love in the process.

Conflict Response Delineator

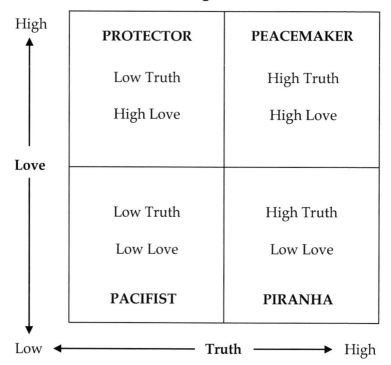

We choose to give truth a high or low priority. We choose to exhibit high or low degrees of love for one another. The degree to which a person exhibits these responses determines their response category.

We will see from more detailed study that individuals can fall into one quadrant at one time and in a different quadrant in a different setting. However, most individuals tend to hover in their comfort zone and respond in ways typical for them. Frequently, their responses are not determined by the truth of the matter, but by their feelings about the issues. When a person is more directly affected by the conflict, they may react with the character traits of the Piranha or the Protector. When less personally affected, they may choose to avoid the fray altogether like a Pacifist, regardless of the consequences for individuals or the church.

As you study the character traits represented by the Conflict Response Delineator, allow God to examine your heart and instruct you, shaping you to demonstrate the ways of the Peacemaker in your life. Which quadrant seems to represent your reaction to conflict most of the time? Are you likely to be a Piranha, Pacifist, Protector, or Peacemaker? Become a Peacemaker and enjoy a harvest of righteousness in your congregation.

The Pacifist

Avoiding conflict, Pacifists often turn a blind eye to their own sin or to the sin of others. They hide out, withdrawing from the fellowship of the church, hoping things will cool down. They wander from the truth, failing to uphold it either in their own lives or in the church. They fail to love others deeply enough to correct them and gently lead them back to the truth. The Pacifist demonstrates low love, low truth.

Ahab, the Evil Pacifist

You will find a few Pacifists running across the pages of scripture, trying to hide from conflict. Ahab, King of Israel, abandoned the truth as did many of his royal predecessors. Having no truth, he was in a weakened position and was unable to influence his notably wicked wife, Jezebel. He was at her bidding, building temples to her gods and following her devious schemes. Ahab relinquished all that God had given him and sold himself to evil (1 Kings 16:29-34; 21:1-14).

Eli, the Priestly Pacifist

Not every Pacifist is evil in thought and deed. Eli was a Levite and a committed priest. His sons became priests also, but his sons were wicked. They had complete disregard for the holiness of the sanctuary where they served and they engaged in immoral activities. Eli was aware of their sin but refused to address it appropriately. His compromise outweighed God's truth and he failed to love his sons enough to correct their deep error. Eventually a prophet, a man of God, confronted Eli with his failures. Because Eli knew the truth but failed to defend it by exercising discipline, God cut short his ministry and the lives of his sons (1 Samuel 2:12-36).

The Corinthian Church, Pacifists All

Churches can be overrun by Pacifists! This was certainly the case in the Corinthian church. Paul discovered that one of the reasons for the discord in their church was an overpopulation of Pacifists. He spoke the truth in love and confronted their gross complacency. One of their church members was involved in sexual immorality and perversion. Paul was incredulous that the church not only condoned the man's activity, but church members became proud of it! They had wandered from truth and failed to love the man enough to help him find his way out of sin (1 Corinthians 5:1-13).

The Protector

Nurturers by nature, Protectors exhibit high degrees of love – or so they believe! Love without truth is a distorted love. Protectors may have such a controlling love that they will go to any length to keep from losing what they hold dear. They can't see that their love is unhealthy and harms more than helps. They become chained to their devotion when they are no longer devoted to the truth. Protectors demonstrate high love, low truth.

Rebekah, the Doting Protector

Rebekah loved Jacob, her second son. However, her love for Jacob overshadowed God's truth about his future. Jacob was second in line for the patriarchal blessing and inheritance. Rachel loved him too much to allow him to come in second. She failed to remember God's promise years earlier that Jacob would become first and that her firstborn would serve his younger brother. Not happy with God's timing and methods, she took matters into her own hands to protect Jacob's interests. Seeking to rob her firstborn of the blessing, she devised a plan to deceive her husband and included her beloved son, Jacob, in the plot (Genesis 27).

Peter, the Mistaken Protector

Christ had just delivered an unsettling message to the disciples. He would have to go to Jerusalem and suffer many things at the hands of religious leaders, including death. Still not quite grasping the truth of Christ's mission, Peter came to Christ's rescue, "'Never, Lord!' he said. 'This shall never happen to you!'" (Matthew 16:22) Jesus immediately spoke the truth in love, "Get behind me, Satan! You are a stumbling block to me; you do not have in mind the things of God, but the things of men" (Matthew 16:23). Christ loved Peter enough to set him straight. Peter was just trying to protect. But protecting Christ was actually an attempt to destroy His mission and that was demonic (Matthew 16:21-26).

The Church of Thyatira, Protector of Evil

The resurrected Christ sent a message to the church in Thyatira through a vision to John. It was a great message at first – "I know your deeds, your love and faith, your service and perseverance" (Revelation 2:19a) – until the big "nevertheless!" A spirit of Jezebel was running amuck, leaving a wake of destruction in its path, filling one woman enough that she caught the attention of the risen Lord. But Christ's chastisement wasn't directed toward her. His correction was aimed at the church's tolerance of her. They protected something evil. They gave her a platform for her foul teaching. Christ longed to see the believers at Thyatira love His Church enough to preserve the truth (Revelation 2:18-29).

The Piranha

The Piranha knows the truth and will defend it to the death – of someone else! They recklessly assert the truth often without a thought to timing or the readiness of someone to hear it. Their words are often harsh and judgmental rather than gentle and redeeming. They act before they think. It is sometimes difficult to correct the Piranha for the very reason that they are speaking truth. They have their facts right, but their delivery lacks love. Piranhas demonstrate low love, high truth.

The Sons of Thunder, Zealous Piranhas

The disciples had a lot to learn. Jesus taught them perfectly, but they didn't pick up His lessons to the same degree of perfection. Jesus was traveling to Jerusalem. He sent messengers ahead into a Samaritan village He would pass through. The messengers were to make preparations for His arrival. However, neither the messengers nor Jesus were welcomed by the villagers. When they discovered He was headed to Jerusalem, they refused to extend an invitation.

Incensed by their lack of hospitality, disciples James and John, the Sons of Thunder, were ready to fly into action. Impressed with some of their recently acquired power, they asked their master, "Lord, do you want us to call fire down from heaven and destroy them?" (Luke 9:54b) Perhaps Jesus was thinking of the woman He had met at the well or others who still needed a big drink of Living Water. Love won out and Jesus turned to rebuke His followers for their rash and unloving thoughts (Luke 9:51-56).

Peter, the Fire-Breathing Piranha

Yes, this is the same man as Peter the Protector. Earlier, we described Peter as loving Christ so much he wanted to spare Jesus any suffering. He didn't rebel against the truth. He didn't understand the truth of Christ's mission. Later, we find the fiery, young disciple in the Garden of Gethsemane as soldiers approach Jesus to arrest Him. Judas gave Jesus the kiss of death and suddenly all the disciples understood what was happening: "When Jesus' followers saw what was going to happen, they said, 'Lord, should we strike with our swords?'" (Luke 22:49) Perhaps Peter asked the question and, without waiting for the answer, drew his sword. Or perhaps the minute the question was posed by another disciple Peter thought, "Great idea!" The Gospel of John throws open the window to Peter's impulsivity, "Then Simon Peter, who had a sword, drew it and struck the high priest's servant, cutting off his right ear." Peter knew the truth. His Teacher was (and still is) the Truth. But Peter's methods were rash, harsh and resulted in injury. Jesus, on the night of his own betrayal, stooped to heal the bleeding servant, demonstrating to Peter the way of the Peacemaker (Luke 22:49-50).

The Church in Ephesus, Peaceful Piranhas

Sometimes Piranhas are content to just swim around, not looking terribly menacing. But remember, the Piranha is low love, high truth. Their lack of love is not always demonstrated through aggressiveness. Such was the case with the church at Ephesus. Once again, we enter John's vision in Revelation. As Jesus walked among the churches, He came to the Beloved Disciple's hometown church. Jesus commends their perseverance in defending truth and outing the false teachers among them. But He gave a strong rebuke to the church as well: "You have forsaken your first love." Christ's arrow of truth hit the bulls-eye. Ephesus was a high truth, low love, kind of church. Since they had lost their passion for Christ, they could not possibly love one another or have compassion for the lost. Truth without love is empty (Revelation 2:1-7).

The Peacemaker

God's Word provides the best description of the Peacemaker: "That they may be encouraged in heart and united in love, so that they may have the full riches of complete understanding, in order that they may know the mystery of God, namely, Christ, in whom are hidden all the treasures of wisdom and knowledge" (Colossians 2:2-3).

Peacemakers abound in love and are completely full of wisdom and knowledge, the Truth. High love, high truth. Understanding the symbiotic relationship of truth and love, Peacemakers know that balance is required or peacemaking is sabotaged. Truth cannot be compromised for the sake of love. Truth without love is empty. When neither truth nor love are present, there is no way to peace, only ruin and misery (Romans 3:16-18). Christ came to show a better way, the ultimate Way, the way of the Peacemaker: High love, high truth.

Jesus, the Prince of Peacemakers

In Christ, our hearts and minds, love and truth, find the perfect balance: "And the peace of God, which transcends all understanding, will guard your hearts and minds in Christ Jesus" (Philippians 4:7). Christ's foundation is truth: "I am the way and the truth and the life. No one comes to the Father except through me" (John 14:6). Truth.

His method is love: "For God so loved the world that He gave His one and only Son, that whoever believes in him shall not perish but have eternal life" (John 3:16). Love.

Christ always confronted falsehood wherever He found it, but His aim was always love and redemption. We have the power within us through the Holy Spirit to confront falsehood and aim for redemption.

The Church of Brotherly Love

The name of the church, Philadelphia, bore witness to believers' deep and sincere love for one another. The word *philadelphia* means brotherly love, or affection for the brothers. The church was struggling and for good reason. They lived in the city of the synagogue of Satan. What a battle for the preservation of truth! Christ's commendation of His Church and the reward He promised her clearly tell us that these Philadelphians held onto the truth, "I know that you have little strength, yet you have kept my word and have not denied my name" (Revelation 3:8). He reassured them that if they could hold on to what they had

– love and truth – a crown would be waiting for them (Revelation 3:7-13).

The Peacemaking Church

Christ still walks among His churches today. When He walks among us, will we be found faithful? Will He see us treading upon the road of peace, holding out the Truth of His Word and loving one another unconditionally?

Paul's prayer for believers in Philippians 1:9-11 shows us the vital connection between love, truth and righteous living that glorifies God:

> And this is my prayer: that your love may abound more and more in knowledge and depth of insight, so that you may be able to discern what is best and may be pure and blameless until the day of Christ, filled with the fruit of righteousness that comes through Jesus Christ – to the glory and praise of God.

Walk in the Spirit

> *These boots are made for walkin',*
> *and that's just what they'll do.*
> *One of these days these boots*
> *are gonna walk all over you!*
> *...Are you ready, boots? Start walkin!'*

Believe it or not, these lyrics were part of a popular song in the 1960s. They reflect much about the culture then and now. When life disappoints, when people betray, shove your feet into a big pair of boots and start walkin' all over somebody. Sadly, this worldly mind-set of retaliation has stomped into more than a few of our churches. Rather than walking in the Spirit, church members stoop to the desires of the flesh, grab their boots and start walkin'!

When conflict embroils a church, peacemakers put on the right shoes and walk in the right way. We learned about the appropriate foot gear in the beginning of this book, when we suited up in the full armor of God preparing for spiritual warfare. There is only one pair of shoes that enable the Peacemaker to face the battles that confront the church: "Therefore put on the full armor of God....with your feet fitted with the readiness that comes from the gospel of peace" (Ephesians 6:13a,15). These shoes are the only ones that fit a believer's feet. A believer who tries to pull on the worldly boots of retaliation looks a bit like Cinderella's stepsisters trying to cram a petite glass slipper on oversized feet. However, when the believer is attired in the full armor of God and wearing the dazzling white robe of Christ's righteousness, only the glass slipper of pure peace will fit perfectly.

Assuming we are now wearing the correct shoes, how should we walk?

No one could offer better walking instructions than the Apostle Paul, who traveled two very different paths in his life. He wore boots of retaliation and stormed down many roads in a murderous rage. In fact, Paul was on the Damascus road, passionately believing he was on the right course. He had the paperwork in hand to storm the places where Christians met and drag them away to their destruction. Paul knew he was right until he encountered Jesus on the same road to Damascus. In one blinding moment, Paul saw the old roadmap of his life contrasted to the new one Jesus set out before him. Then he knew he had been wrong. Dead wrong. He was on the right road, but he was going the wrong way! (Acts 9, 26)

When Paul met Jesus, his direction, beliefs, attitudes, actions, and heart were all radically changed. He exchanged his heavy boots of hatred and retaliation for a pair of shoes that fit perfectly for carrying the gospel of peace to the world. Once Paul experienced the life and light of Jesus, he had a new way of walking and he wanted others to know about it. He wanted to empower Christians by showing them how to "walk in the Spirit."

Walk According to the Spirit

Think of the way a baby learns to walk. First he clings to furniture, taking one tentative step at a time. As his confidence grows and his muscles strengthen, he soon leaves the security of holding on to something. He lets go and darts forward with exuberance, having discovered a new freedom. The only way to go forward is to let go.

Understanding the Christian walk, Paul teaches believers how to let go of the old ways of life and press forward to a new freedom, the freedom in Christ. We are free to leave our old nature behind and run with eagerness to go where the Holy Spirit leads. As the following points indicate, Romans 8:5-16 is Paul's instruction book on how to walk according to the Spirit.

- We are alive in the Spirit! We experience a new life in Christ - the old life is dead (Romans 8:10).

- Each day we live by the Spirit constantly putting to death the misdeeds of our flesh (Romans 8:13).

- We are authenticated by the Spirit – His presence in our lives proves we are God's children (Romans 8:16).

- We let the Spirit shape our desires. Our desires are never contrary to the Spirit's desires (Romans 8:5).

- We are led by the Spirit, not human plans or emotions (Romans 8:14).

- No longer controlled by our sinful natures, we are controlled by the Spirit because the Holy Spirit lives in us (Romans 8:9).

Our whole approach to life is altered when we walk according to the Spirit. It is no different when we experience church conflict. We no longer react to conflict like unbelievers. We won't assert our way of handling things or our way of achieving our desired outcome. As peacemakers, we desire only what the Spirit desires and we will wait upon the Spirit to show us the way (Romans 8:5). We are no longer controlled by the sinful nature (Galatians 5:16, 19-21) We surrender to the control of the Spirit. He is the one directing our every step and decision (Romans 8:9).

When we walk by the Spirit through conflict, we are not startled as though awakened by an intruder in the middle of the night. We are alive in the Spirit, constantly alert and ready for action (Romans 8:10, 1 Peter 5:8). We put on the shoes of peace to confront conflict rather than rashly pulling on the boots of retaliation. With peace as our mission, the Spirit will lead us, and we will see life rising through the ashes of turmoil (Romans 8:13-14). Finally, we prove that we are God's children when we approach conflict by walking according to the Spirit (Romans 8:16).

Walk as Jesus Did

Three preteen girls from Light on the Hill Church decided to go to the church gym while a fellowship dinner was in progress. Sneaking to their destination through dim hallways made the way more mysterious and exciting. They opened the gym door and let it close slowly behind them. Engulfed in absolute darkness, the girls stood motionless and silent. They had never experienced such darkness. They literally could not see their hands in front of their faces.

To break the silence, one of the girls came up with a rather foolhardy idea. She dared the others to start running as fast as they could in the pitch blackness. The first girl launched out about ten feet and would go no farther. The second girl, flailing her arms wildly, ran about thirty feet before stumbling over some equipment on the floor. The daredevil in the group thought she was the bravest of all and wanted to prove it. She ran at top speed, but unable to judge distance in the darkness, crashed into the opposite wall of the gym. Laughter and tears all ran together into near hysteria.

Breathlessly the girls called out to one another and managed to regroup. They held hands and slowly made their way back to the hall navigating by a thin slice of light under the door. Now the dim light of the hallway seemed bright. Squinting their eyes they quickly steered a course straight back to the fellowship dinner.

We can readily see that these girls were unwise to play such a dangerous game. Yet we engage in similar behaviors by planning our own courses through conflict. Finding ourselves engulfed in the darkness of conflict, we decide to run headlong into the black without consulting God's Word or accessing the light of Christ's Spirit.

> Watch out that you do not lose what you have worked for, but that you may be rewarded fully. Anyone who runs ahead and does not continue in the teaching of Christ does not have God; whoever continues in the teaching has both the Father and the Son.
>
> 2 John 1:8-9

We know that we have come to know him if we obey his commands. The man who says, "I know him," but does not do what he commands is a liar, and the truth is not in him. But if anyone obeys his word, God's love is truly made complete in him. This is how we know we are in him: Whoever claims to live in him must walk as Jesus did (1 John 2:3-6).

If we claim to know Christ, to be his followers, we must walk as Jesus walked. The Greek word for walk is *peripateo* which means "to conduct one's life." To walk as Jesus walked is to conduct ourselves just like the Prince of Peace did! Not doing so makes us liars. We are to emulate Christ's attitudes and character when conflict arises. We either walk like Jesus walked or we are running ahead in the dark.

Conflict in church is difficult. However, we are never given license to abandon all that Christ teaches by running ahead of Him and handling matters our own way. We stand to lose much when we run off course. All that we have done to build unity in the body of Christ can be wrecked by mishandling one conflict. We are to know God's Word and continue in it, no matter how the circumstances around us change. When we continue in the Word, walking as Christ did, our reward is amazing.

Christ admonished the church of Sardis in Revelation 3:1-6. He told them their reputation for being alive was false. They had fallen asleep. They were holding on by a thread. Only a few had remained constant to Christ's teaching. He then describes the wonderful reward for the faithful, "Yet you have a few people in Sardis who have not soiled their clothes. They will walk with me, dressed in white, for they are worthy" (Revelation 3:4). If we walk as Jesus walked while we are members of His Church, we will walk in a manner worthy of the Lord, we will please him and we will bear fruit (Colossians 1:9b-10).

Let us then walk with Christ through any fires of conflict, seek His solutions, be filled with the knowledge of His will, with His spiritual wisdom and His understanding. What a joy to know that we would be so pleasing to Christ by being peacemakers that He would throw a white robe over our shoulders and walk with us along heaven's streets.

Keep Step with the Spirit

We've learned how to walk as peacemakers, to walk according to the Spirit and to walk as Jesus did. Now let us keep in step and not lag behind. We've examined several ways the Holy Spirit enables us to throw off our natural, sinful inclinations and be filled with the fruit of the Spirit – joy, love, peace, patience, kindness, goodness, faithfulness, gentleness, and self-control (Galatians 5:22-23). We don't bear these fruits only when calmness prevails or when it's easy to harvest them in our lives. We bear the fruit of the Spirit when times are difficult or impossible. Even during times of trouble, we can dig deeply into the fertile soil where the Spirit of Christ has changed our hearts, has made us new creations, and we find the power to exude Christ's character. Christ never operated under the circumstances. He lived above them in power and victory. We can do the same if we walk according to the Spirit, walk as Jesus did and continue to keep in step with the Spirit.

Paul warned the Galatians about what was causing them to lag behind, "You foolish Galatians! Who has bewitched you? Are you so foolish? After beginning with the Spirit, are you now trying to attain your goal by human effort?" (Galatians 3:1a,3) We can't achieve salvation by our own effort,

> Since we live by the Spirit, let us keep in step with the Spirit.
> *Galatians 5:25*

we can't bear fruit by our own effort and we can't resolve conflict by our own effort. Only as we exemplify the ways of a peacemaker through the power of the Holy Spirit can we properly glorify God, stay focused on Christ, speak the truth in love, and walk in the Spirit.

As a final word of instruction in walking by the Spirit, read Paul's exhortation to the Philippians, the roadmap for the peacemaker:

> If you have any encouragement from being united with Christ, if any comfort from his love, if any fellowship with the Spirit, if any tenderness and compassion, then make my joy complete by being like-minded, having the same love, being one in spirit and purpose. Do nothing out of selfish ambition or vain conceit, but in humility consider others better than yourselves. Each of you should look not only to your own interests, but also to the interests of others. Your attitude should be the same as that of Christ Jesus. Do everything without complaining or arguing, so that you may become blameless and pure, children of God...in which you shine like stars in the universe as you hold out the word of life (Philippians 2:1-5, 14-16a).

Remain Steadfast

Not every mile of a marathon is grueling. Experienced runners know that the first half of a marathon is relatively easy. Many runners visit, laugh and wave at spectators during the early miles of a race. After the halfway point, though, the race becomes serious. As one running expert writes,

> Even the best-trained runners start to hurt....the next few miles might be described as demanding, maybe taxing. The miles after that [are] hard [and] punishing. Past 20 miles almost everyone starts to struggle. [These miles are]

backbreaking, rough, and harsh on the
Grueling Scale. But...those final 385 yards?
They can be severe; but they also can be spirit-
lifting. Anybody who has stood beside the
finish line of a marathon understands that.[45]

The Race Before Us

Whether or not you realize it, we're running a
marathon. We're in a lifelong race that has a finish line at
the feet of Jesus. The Apostle Paul describes this glorious
destination by writing:

> I have fought the good fight, I have finished the
> race, I have kept the faith. Now there is in store
> for me the crown of righteousness, which the
> Lord, the righteous Judge, will award to me on
> that day – and not only to me, but also to all
> who have longed for his appearing (2 Timothy
> 4:7-8).

Paul's life was consumed by the desire to finish the
race well. He wrote, "I consider my life worth nothing to
me, if only I may finish the race and complete the task the
Lord Jesus has given me - the task of testifying to the
gospel of God's grace" (Acts 20:24). Nothing else really
mattered to Paul – not hardship, persecution, or even the
threat of death. What is your passionate, all-consuming
desire? Anything less than faithfully fulfilling God's
calling in your life will not sustain you through troubled
times.

Run to Win!

A runner once remarked, "Some people run a
marathon for enjoyment or to raise money. Other people

want to see how fast they can run. I run to win." Why not run to win? Why settle for anything less for our lives and churches? Paul certainly had a winning outlook on his ministry and life, and he encouraged every Christian to have the same perspective: "Don't you realize that in a race everyone runs, but only one person gets the prize? So run to win! All athletes are disciplined in their training. They do it to win a prize that will fade away, but we do it for an eternal prize" (1 Corinthians 9:24-25, NLT).

Dropping Out

It's easy to begin a race. Nearly everyone begins well but only a few finish well. Regrettably, not all of us are willing to discipline our lives to win the race that God has set for us. Some people are content to have a superficial relationship with Christ during the easy times of life, neglecting God's Word, prayer and ministry. When difficulties inevitably come into their lives and churches, they're unequipped to persevere. They choose to leave their churches, nursing their wounds and taking all their unresolved issues to another congregation. Or they may drop out of church altogether.

It's disheartening to discover how many people leave their churches when conflict erupts. One survey found that nearly 40 percent of the church members and pastors who leave their congregations do so because of conflict.[46] Rather than "run the race" that God has called them to with perseverance and commitment, many Christians choose the easiest option and simply leave their churches. Common reasons for this choice include:

- A superficial or nonexistent relationship with Christ

- A consumer mentality that encourages people to leave their churches when conflict creates discomfort and disrupts what they receive from church

- An unrealistic view of human sin that overlooks the fact that people will bring their personal problems into the life of the congregation

- Failure to follow biblical guidelines for interpersonal and congregational peacemaking

- Broken relationships

- Impatience

- Discouragement

Shawn and Meredith remembered how excited they were when they became the outreach directors for their church. Several other church members had volunteered to help them reach out to their community in new and creative ways. For the first time in years the Lighthouse Community Church was truly reaching those who needed to receive the gospel of Jesus Christ.

The outreach ministry grew as church members began to see how God was using Shawn and Meredith's leadership to mobilize the congregation for evangelism. However, dissension among outreach team members began to surface as some people expressed concern about Shawn's strong personality. His "Type A" personality was highly productive but sometimes too strong for a few people. Rather than come to Shawn with their concerns, these individuals began to talk about him behind his back. Frustrated by the

> Therefore, since we are surrounded by such a great cloud of witnesses, let us throw off everything that hinders and the sin that so easily entangles, and let us run with perseverance the race marked out for us. Let us fix our eyes on Jesus.
> *Hebrews 12:1-2a*

ways he was being attacked, Shawn asked the pastor for help. However, months passed and no one, not even the pastor, could get to the bottom of the matter.

Shawn and Meredith couldn't take the pressure any longer. Even though the outreach ministry was seeing tremendous results and a clear majority of the people were supportive of their leadership, Shawn and Meredith decided to leave their ministry and the church. They were hurt and discouraged, and nothing that the pastor could say would change their decision.

Run with Perseverance!

Running a marathon is challenging for even a seasoned, disciplined athlete. Miles 13 to 20 of the 26.2 mile run are hard and punishing. After mile 20 every muscle is on fire, legs feel like Jell-O, hands can go numb. The final stretch is incredibly difficult, yet as the finish line comes into sight, everything changes. Winning the race – even just finishing the race – makes all the sacrifice and suffering worthwhile.

The New Testament uses the Greek word *hupomone* to describe how we are called to run the race with perseverance and endurance. The word literally means "to remain under" the trials and difficulties of life. Rather than try to get out from under them as quickly as possible to be relieved of their pressure, we are called to remain steadfast and refuse to succumb to our circumstances. We focus on what is beyond our current troubles, fixing our eyes on Jesus (Hebrews 12:1-2a), holding fast to God's calling on our lives (2 Thessalonians 1:11), and remembering Christ's example, "who for the joy

> Therefore, my dear brothers, stand firm. Let nothing move you. Always give yourselves fully to the work of the Lord, because you know that your labor in the Lord is not in vain.
> *1 Corinthians 15:58*

set before him endured [*hupomeno*] the cross" (Hebrews 12:2b).

God does not call us to passively resign ourselves to difficult situations with a "woe is me," self-pitying attitude. We persevere courageously and triumphantly, strengthened by our certain and vibrant faith in Christ.

Can we remain steadfast in our own strength? Absolutely not! We persevere as we allow God to strengthen and mature us spiritually through church conflict. As the following passages indicate, learning to trust in God's power to transform difficult circumstances is an ongoing process:

> Consider it pure joy, my brothers, whenever you face trials of many kinds, because you know that the testing of your faith develops perseverance. Perseverance must finish its work so that you may be mature and complete, not lacking anything (James 1:2-4).

> Not only so, but we also rejoice in our sufferings, because we know that suffering produces perseverance; perseverance, character; and character, hope (Romans 5:3-4).

Don't Grow Weary

Facing the trials of church conflict with perseverance depends on our passion to glorify God, to stay focused on Christ, to hold fast to truth and love, and to walk steadfastly in the Spirit. We have Christ's own example of endurance in the face of incredibly intense conflict

> Consider him [Christ] who endured such opposition from sinful men, so that you will not grow weary and lose heart.
> *Hebrews 12:3*

and opposition. Today He offers us the strength of His own endurance as we face our challenges.

We can be certain that when times are troubled, God is not. He will display His glory. He will guide our footsteps. He will meet us when we cross the finish line.

One night after a grueling day of facing conflicts in the church, the young pastor and his wife sat on their patio. Holding his hand, his wife searched his eyes. "Will we survive this?" she asked. They both looked up to the heavens, to the expanse of God's creation. "Yes," he answered, "We will survive, and God will be glorified. That's our prize! It's worth the struggle." They sat quietly, feeling peace in the night and peace in their hearts.

When we choose to remain steadfast, we give God the opportunity to work in our lives and congregations. We give God the opportunity to build our faith. We give our churches the opportunity to become the beautiful Bride of Christ. We give people who are outside the faith and the church an opportunity to see God's supernatural, reconciling love. And, most importantly, we have the opportunity to glorify our great and marvelous God.

Soli Deo Gloria.

Glory to God alone.

Glory to God "in the church and
in Christ Jesus throughout all generations,
for ever and ever!"

(Ephesians 3:21)

Scriptures for Resolving Conflict

Engage in church practices that promote congregational health and growth

The best way to prevent church conflict is to develop healthy, biblical relationships in your congregation. These relationships do not develop accidentally. They require time, even years, to cultivate. A climate of peace is the result of an intentional churchwide discipleship process that leads believers to spiritual maturity and includes teaching principles of biblical peacemaking. Healthy relationships among church members are encouraged by the ways leaders model godly behavior and responses to conflict. Positive, peacemaking relationships among believers will establish a positive climate in your church, replacing sinful, dysfunctional responses to conflict with the fruit of God's Spirit: love, joy, peace, patience, kindness, goodness, faithfulness, gentleness, and self-control (Galatians 5:22-23a).

Actively engage in discipleship that leads to spiritual growth, maturity, and stability

> It was [Christ] who gave some to be apostles, some to be prophets, some to be evangelists, and some to be pastors and teachers, to prepare God's people for works of service, so that the body of Christ may be built up until we all reach unity in the faith and in the knowledge of the Son of God and become mature, attaining to the whole measure of the fullness of Christ. Then we will no longer be infants, tossed back and forth by the waves, and blown here and there by every wind of teaching and by the cunning and craftiness of men in their deceitful scheming. Instead, speaking the truth in love, we will in

all things grow up into him who is the Head, that is, Christ (Ephesians 4:11-15).

Encourage church members to follow the example of godly spiritual leaders

Remember your leaders, who spoke the word of God to you. Consider the outcome of their way of life and imitate their faith (Hebrews 13:7).

Foster positive, peacemaking relationships among church members

As a prisoner for the Lord, then, I urge you to live a life worthy of the calling you have received. Be completely humble and gentle; be patient, bearing with one another in love (Ephesians 4:1-2).

Therefore encourage one another and build each other up, just as in fact you are doing (1 Thessalonians 5:11, NASB).

Therefore, accept one another, just as Christ also accepted us to the glory of God (Romans 15:7, NASB).

And let us consider how we may spur one another on toward love and good deeds (Hebrews 10:24).

May the God who gives endurance and encouragement give you a spirit of unity among yourselves as you follow Christ Jesus, so that with one heart and mouth you may glorify the God and Father of our Lord Jesus Christ (Romans 15:5-6).

Conflict is inevitable, so be prepared!

Interpersonal conflict is as old as Cain and Abel. While creating a climate of peace will greatly reduce the amount and severity of conflict in your church, conflict is inevitable. It's one consequence of living in a fallen, sinful world.

Jesus promised that His followers will experience trouble

> I have told you these things, so that in me you may have peace. In this world you will have trouble. But take heart! I have overcome the world (John 16:33).

The New Testament record provides several examples of conflict in the early church

> In those days when the number of disciples was increasing, the Grecian Jews among them complained against the Hebraic Jews because their widows were being overlooked in the daily distribution of food (Acts 6:1).

> Some men came down from Judea to Antioch and were teaching the brothers: "Unless you are circumcised, according to the custom taught by Moses, you cannot be saved." This brought Paul and Barnabas into sharp dispute and debate with them (Acts 15:1-2a).

> [Paul and Barnabas] had such a sharp disagreement that they parted company (Acts 15:39a).

> My brothers, some from Chloe's household have informed me that there are quarrels among you (1 Corinthians 1:11).

> I [Paul] plead with Euodia and I plead with Syntyche to agree with each other in the Lord (Philippians 4:2).

> To the twelve tribes scattered among the nations....What causes fights and quarrels among you?... You quarrel and fight (James 1:1, 4:1-2).

When a conflict consists of little more than a mild disagreement, it can usually be resolved with minimal effort (i.e., agreeing to disagree in godly ways). The "Lead Your Church through Conflict" workshop by Building Healthy Churches® describes four other stages of conflict that threaten the unity and witness of our churches. Each stage is described along with suggestions for effective interventions by church leaders.

Remember the real sources of conflict

Other people are not our adversaries. Satan has declared war against us and our churches. He's our avowed enemy who is waiting for just the right time and place to attack. Because God has defeated Satan on the cross of Christ (Colossians 2:15) and is sovereign over Satan, God limits what Satan can do (Job 1:12; Luke 22:31-32). Satan cannot destroy believers or the Church of Jesus Christ. However, he can render us and our congregations ineffective for the gospel of Christ by inciting sinful attitudes and actions that destroy our unity and witness.

When conflict erupts in your church, remember that it is a spiritual conflict that must be resolved using spiritual means. Remember that Satan attacks congregations directly or appeals to our weaknesses and/or spiritual immaturity to fulfill his diabolical schemes.

Acknowledge that Satan is our real foe

> For our struggle is not against flesh and blood, but against the rulers, against the authorities, against the powers of this dark world and against the spiritual forces of evil in the heavenly realms (Ephesians 6:12).

Be self-controlled and alert. Your enemy the devil prowls around like a roaring lion looking for someone to devour (1 Peter 5:8).

[Satan is] the accuser of our brethren (Revelation 12:10).

Recognize the power of sin in our lives

What causes fights and quarrels among you? Don't they come from your desires that battle within you? (James 4:1)

Identify the destructive consequences of spiritual immaturity

Brothers, I could not address you as spiritual but as worldly – mere infants in Christ.... For since there is jealousy and quarreling among you, are you not worldly? (1 Corinthians 3:1-3)

Examine your attitudes and motives

Our inner life matters to God. He cares little for our outward appearances but is intensely concerned with the condition of our hearts. He searches our hearts – the place no one else can see – and calls us to confess any sinful attitudes and motives.

Conduct a heart check

Do nothing from selfishness or empty conceit, but with humility of mind regard one another as more important than yourselves; do not merely look out for your own personal interests, but also for the interests of others (Philippians 2:3-4, NASB).

You have heard that it was said to the people long ago, "Do not murder, and anyone who murders will be subject to judgment." But I tell you that anyone who is angry with his brother will be subject to judgment. Again, anyone who says to his brother, "Raca," is answerable to the Sanhedrin. But anyone who says, "You fool!" will be in danger of the fire of hell (Matthew 5:21-22).

Create in me a pure heart, O God, and renew a steadfast spirit within me (Psalm 51:10).

Remove log jams

Why do you look at the speck of sawdust in your brother's eye and pay no attention to the plank in your own eye? How can you say to your brother, "Let me take the speck out of your eye," when all the time there is a plank in your own eye? You hypocrite, first take the plank out of your own eye, and then you will see clearly to remove the speck from your brother's eye (Matthew 7:3-5).

If we confess our sins, he is faithful and just and will forgive us our sins and purify us from all unrighteousness (1 John 1:9).

Glorify God

...whatever you do, do all to the glory of God (1 Corinthians 10:31, NASB).

Put on the full armor of God

The armor of God enables us to "stand firm" against Satan's attacks and have an effective, vibrant spiritual life and witness. Believers are not hapless victims of Satan's wiles; he can and should be defeated daily by employing the...

- absolute truth of God's Word, the Bible

- righteousness which comes through Christ

- certainty that comes from experiencing and sharing the gospel of peace

- protection brought by steadfast faith in the promises of God

- security that comes from a salvation that is completely of God

- power of God's Word that "penetrates even to dividing soul and spirit, joints and marrow; it judges the thoughts and attitudes of the heart" (Hebrews 4:12).

- connection that comes from an active and vital prayer life

Therefore put on the full armor of God, so that when the day of evil comes, you may be able to stand your ground, and after you have done everything, to stand. Stand firm then, with the belt of truth buckled around your waist, with the breastplate of righteousness in place, and with your feet fitted with the readiness that comes from the gospel of peace. In addition to all this, take up the shield of faith, with which you can extinguish all the flaming arrows of the evil one. Take the helmet of salvation and the sword of the Spirit, which is the word of God. And pray in the Spirit on all occasions with all kinds of prayers and requests. With this in mind, be alert and always keep on praying for all the saints (Ephesians 6:13-18).

Offer grace

Have others wronged you? To forgive is to offer grace (undeserved favor) to those who have wronged us. Forgiveness involves our conscious, unilateral decision to reject the desire to make others pay for what they've done to us. Forgiveness changes our hearts and desires for God to work in those who have wronged us, bringing His judgment, discipline, and grace into their lives. As Peter Barnes has written, "Forgiveness is an act of faith. By forgiving another person, I am simply trusting that God is better at justice than I am, and I leave the issues of fairness to Him to work out. Wrong does not disappear when I forgive, but it does lose its grip on me, and God is able to redeem the brokenness of life" (Peter Barnes, "Learning to Live into Forgiveness and Grace: Sermon Series on the Book of Genesis [Genesis 33:1-20]," available from http://www.fpcboulder.org/ transcripts /4-27-03.html#_edn3. Used by permission.)

Forgive as God forgave you

> Let all bitterness and wrath and anger and clamor and slander be put away from you, along with all malice. Be kind to one another, tender-hearted, forgiving each other, just as God in Christ has also forgiven you (Ephesians 4:31-32, NASB).

> Bear with each other and forgive whatever grievances you may have against one another. Forgive as the Lord forgave you (Colossians 3:13).

> Then Peter came to Jesus and asked, "Lord, how many times shall I forgive my brother when he sins against me? Up to seven times?" Jesus answered, "I tell you, not

seven times, but seventy-seven times" (Matthew 18:21-22).

Above all, love each other deeply, because love covers over a multitude of sins (1 Peter 4:8).

Pursue reconciliation

Forgiveness transforms our hearts as we offer to others what we have received through Jesus Christ. Reconciliation occurs when others accept our forgiveness. This mends our broken relationships and restores our fellowship with one another. Forgiveness is unconditional and unilateral; reconciliation, however, depends on the response of others. The Bible teaches that we must go to great lengths to seek reconciliation with our brothers and sisters in Christ.

Take the initiative

If it is possible, as far as it depends on you, live at peace with everyone (Romans 12:18).

Therefore if you are presenting your offering at the altar, and there remember that your brother has something against you, leave your offering there before the altar and go; first be reconciled to your brother, and then come and present your offering (Matthew 5:23-24, NASB).

If your brother sins, go and show him his fault in private (Matthew 18:15a).

Make every effort

Let us therefore make every effort to do what leads to peace and to mutual edification (Romans 14:19).

Make every effort to keep the unity of the Spirit through the bond of peace (Ephesians 4:3).

Restore gently

Brethren, even if anyone is caught in any trespass, you who are spiritual, restore such a one in a spirit of gentleness; each one looking to yourself, so that you too will not be tempted (Galatians 6:1, NASB).

The Lord's bond-servant must not be quarrelsome, but be kind to all, able to teach, patient when wronged, with gentleness correcting those who are in opposition, if perhaps God may grant them repentance leading to the knowledge of the truth, and they may come to their senses and escape from the snare of the devil, having been held captive by him to do his will (2 Timothy 2:24-26, NASB).

Confront incrementally

If your brother sins, go and show him his fault in private; if he listens to you, you have won your brother. But if he does not listen to you, take one or two more with you, so that by the mouth of two or three witnesses every fact may be confirmed. If he refuses to listen to them, tell it to the church; and if he refuses to listen to the church, let him be to you as a Gentile and a tax collector. Truly I say to you, whatever you bind on earth shall have been bound in heaven; and whatever you loose on earth shall have been loosed in heaven (Matthew 18:15-18, NASB).

Warn a divisive person once, and then warn him a second time. After that, have nothing to do with him. You may be sure that such a man is warped and sinful; he is self-condemned (Titus 3:10-11).

Trust God

Reconciliation might happen quickly or not as soon as we would like for it to happen. Either way, we can place our absolute confidence in God's timing, purposes, and ways. He is in control of our circumstances, and Christ is Lord of our lives, churches, and yes, even conflicts! We must trust the God who has lavished His love upon us (1 John 3:1) and the Savior who sacrificially gave Himself for the Church (Ephesians 5:25-27).

> But I tell you: Love your enemies and pray for those who persecute you (Matthew 5:44).

> ...the Lord disciplines those he loves... (Hebrews 12:6).

> Do not take revenge, my friends, but leave room for God's wrath, for it is written: "It is mine to avenge; I will repay," says the Lord. On the contrary: "If your enemy is hungry, feed him; if he is thirsty, give him something to drink. In doing this, you will heap burning coals on his head." Do not be overcome by evil, but overcome evil with good (Romans 12:19-21).

Using this Resource in Your Church

Church Conflict by the Book is designed to help church leaders and members avoid destructive conflict in their congregations. This book is based on the premise that a biblical understanding of personal discipleship, church health and proactive peacemaking enables congregations to develop a shared perspective on conflict that will greatly reduce or eliminate its destructive effects. *Church Conflict by the Book* seeks to equip congregations to become spiritually healthy and effective in carrying out the Great Commission.

A downloadable group discussion guide is available for this book at www.churchconflictbythebook.com. Churches across America have used this helpful resource with the book for leadership training, during the transition between pastors, as a churchwide study, and in small groups. Comments about *Church Conflict by the Book* following a group study include the following statements:

> *Church Conflict by the Book* has mesmerized the people in our home Bible study group as we search for the Holy Spirit's leading through challenging times in our local church. We are experiencing inner healing and a powerful new fellowship through the Bible-based teaching and spiritual wisdom of this study. The book leaves us chastened, matured and with great hope for holding our church together during troubled times.

> Seventy of our church members are excitedly going through *Church Conflict by the Book*. Presently we are experiencing a calm and happy time in our church. However, we know that Satan does not

like a happy congregation and that is why we are doing this study. *Church Conflict by the Book* strikes directly at the heart of church conflict and answers many of our questions regarding how to stand against Satan's attacks. We are very thankful for this resource and know it will benefit our church for many years to come. It is a "must" Bible study for every congregation!

Our study group has just finished reading and discussing the fourth chapter of the book. It was so good that we had a difficult time stopping. As a matter of fact, we couldn't finish all the activities in the study guide because of all the discussion. Everyone is enjoying the book and is always eager to start reading for the next week. It's changing their hearts and lives. As chairman of the deacons I plan to use *Church Conflict by the Book* in our next training class for new deacons.

I think *Church Conflict by the Book* is an excellent study on a topic that is rarely addressed so directly in other materials. We plan to use this book as a small group study this fall. We hope it will be helpful in a church which has experienced a great deal of strife in the last 10 years.

Church Conflict by the Book has applied to several situations in my life outside of church, especially at work. Now I know how to deal with difficult people on the job, extending God's grace and forgiveness to them...and it's really making a difference!

This book really made me stop and think about the behaviors I need to change in my own life.

I thoroughly enjoyed the study and the interaction in our small group. *Church Conflict by the Book* was an excellent learning experience that strengthened personal relationships in our church.

Every church of every denomination should read this book, especially those in leadership positions.

Church Conflict by the Book is very thorough and well put together. It helped me to see previous church conflicts in a new light and equipped me to deal with present and future conflicts. The truths taught in the book also applied in many ways to my personal and social life.

The book's greatest value to me was (1) the consistent and repeated direction to self-examination and (2) the emphasis on "intentional love" vs. loving those who earn it. The highlighted examples of church conflicts throughout the book were helpful and illuminating.

Everyone in our church should read this book!

Church Conflict by the Book is simply "life-changing." Now I understand how God expects us to resolve church conflict. My walk with God is closer and my relationships with other believers are better. I think our church should offer this book to church members once a year!

Endnotes

[1] The scenarios used in this book are based on actual events but the names of individuals and churches are fictitious.

[2] Unless otherwise indicated, scripture references are from the HOLY BIBLE, NEW INTERNATIONAL VERSION®. NIV®. Copyright © 1973, 1978, 1984 by International Bible Society.

[3] Simon J. Kistemaker, *New Testament Commentary: Exposition of James, John, Peter, and Jude* (Grand Rapids, MI: Baker Books, 1996), 130.

[4] Ron Susek, *Firestorm: Preventing and Overcoming Church Conflicts* (Grand Rapids, MI: Baker Books, 1999), 105.

[5] Monty Hale, "Peacemaker Confab Designed to Resolve Church Conflict," *The Pathway*, 21 December 2004, 4.

[6] Susek, *Firestorm*, 52.

[7] Eric Reed, "Leadership Surveys Church Conflict," *Christianity Today*; available from http://www.ctlibrary.com/le/2004/fall/6.25.html.

[8] Susek, *Firestorm*, 111.

[9] Peter Barnes, "Learning to Live into Forgiveness and Grace: Sermon Series on the Book of Genesis (Genesis 33:1-20)"; available from http://www.fpcboulder.org/transcripts/4-27-03.html#_edn3. Used by permission.

[10] Ibid.

[11] Taken *from The Purpose Driven Life: What on Earth Am I Here For?* by Rick Warren. Copyright © 2002 by Rick Warren. Used by permission of Zondervan, www.zondervan .com.

[12] Rick Warren, "Breaking through the Attendance Barrier," Ministry Toolbox, Issue 109 (July 2, 2003); available from http://www.pastors.com/RWMT/default.asp?id=109 &artid=4353&expand=1.

[13] Roy Gane, *Leviticus, Numbers, The NIV Application Commentary* (Grand Rapids, MI: Zondervan, 2004), 603.

[14] Ibid., 602.

[15] Ibid., 636.

[16] Ibid.

[17] The titles of "overseer" and "elder" are used interchangeably in the Bible, referring to the same office (Acts 20:17,28; Titus 1:5,7; 1 Peter 5:1-2). They became misconstrued later in church history to refer to two separate offices - that of bishop and elder. Alexander Strauch, *Biblical Eldership: An Urgent Call to Restore Biblical Church Leadership, Revised and Expanded* (Littleton, CO: Lewis and Roth Publisher, 1995), 179.

[18] The Greek word for "deacon" is *diakonos*, which, depending on its context, can be translated as a "servant, helper or official of the church." Walter Bauer, *A Greek-English Lexicon of the New Testament and Other Early Christian Literature,* 2d ed., revised and augmented by F. Wilbur Gingrich and Frederick W. Danker (Chicago, IL: The University of Chicago Press, 1979), 184. Many biblical commentators believe that the seven men who were selected for practical service in the early church (Acts 6:1-7) were the forerunners of those who later held the office of deacon described in Philippians 1:1 and 1 Timothy 3:8-13. As evidenced by the preaching of Stephen (Acts 7) and the evangelism of

Philip (Acts 8), the ministry of deacons includes both spiritual and practical ministries.

[19] David Johnson and Jeff VanVonderen, *The Subtle Power of Spiritual Abuse: Recognize and Escaping Spiritual Manipulation and False Spiritual Authority within the Church* (Minneapolis, MN: Bethany House Publishers, 1991), 23.

[20] Ibid., 24.

[21] Reprinted by permission. *"Under Cover: The Promise of Protection under His Authority,* John Bevere, 2001, Thomas Nelson Inc. Nashville, Tennessee. All rights reserved," 134.

[22] Reprinted by permission. *"Under Cover: The Promise of Protection under His Authority, Participant's Guide,* John Bevere, 2001, Thomas Nelson Inc. Nashville, Tennessee. All rights reserved," 126.

[23] "The word which Luke has chosen to describe the disagreement between Paul and Barnabas originally meant 'an irritation,' but in this context something much stronger is indicated, that is, a sharp argument." Barclay M. Newman and Eugene Nida, *A Translator's Handbook on the Acts of the Apostles* (London, England: United Bible Societies, 1972), 306.

[24] Ken Sande, "Strike the Shepherd – Losing Pastors in the Church"; available from http://www.peacemaker.net/site/c.aqKFLTOBIpH/b.1084141/apps/nl/content3.asp?content_id=%7B7A3375ED-91B4-4CC9-91D0-228B9375D2C2%7D&notoc=1. Used by permission.

[25] John MacArthur, "A Practical Guide for Disciples: Sheep among Wolves – Part 2," message 2280, 1981; available from http://www.biblebb.com/files/MAC/sg2280.htm.

26 John Franklin and Chuck Lawless, *Spiritual Warfare: Biblical Truth for Victory* (Nashville, TN: LifeWay Press, 2001), 75.

27 William Barclay, *Letters to the Seven Churches* (New York: Abingdon Press, 1958, c1957), 60.

28 Jimmy Draper quoted in an article by Brian Koonce, "MBC Preaching Conference Emphasizes Acting Like Jesus, Preaching Jesus," *The Pathway*, 19 December 2006, 8.

29 Bill O'Reilly. Website: www.billoreilly.com.

30 *The American Heritage® Dictionary of the English Language*, Fourth Edition (Boston, MA: Houghton Mifflin Company, 2006); available on http://dictionary.reference.com/browse/bloviate.

31 Kent Crockett, *I Once Was Blind But Now I Squint* (Chattanooga, TN: AMG Publishers, 2004), 94.

32 Aubrey Malphurs, *Being Leaders: The Nature of Authentic Christian Leadership* (Grand Rapids, MI: Baker Books, 2003), 179.

33 Ibid., 178-179.

34 Ibid., 123.

35 John Piper, "Letter to a Friend Concerning the So-Called 'Lordship Salvation'" (1 February 1990); available on http://www.desiringgod.org/ResourceLibrary/Articles/ByDate/1990/1496_ Letter_to_a_Friend_Concerning_the_So_Called_Lordship_ Salvation/; By John Piper © Desiring God. Website: www.desiringGod.org. Email: mail@desiringGod.org. Toll Free: 1.888.346.4700.

36 Henry T. Blackaby and Richard Blackaby, *Experiencing God Day-By-Day: The Devotional Journal* (Nashville, TN: Broadman & Holman Publishers, 1998), 184.

37 Bevere,, *Under Cover*, 88.

38 Ibid.

39 Ibid., 87-88.

40 Ibid., 134.

41 Bevere, *Under Cover, Participant's Guide,* 126.

42 John MacArthur, Romans 9-16, *The MacArthur New Testament Commentary* (Chicago, IL: The Moody Bible Institute of Chicago, 1994), 203.

43 Bernhard W. Anderson, *Understanding the Old Testament*, Fourth Edition (Englewood Cliffs, NJ: Prentice Hall, 1986), 308.

44 See Job chapters 38-41.

45 Hal Higdon, "Is Running a Marathon Grueling?" (2005); available at http://halhigdon.com/ Ontherun/ marathongrueling.htm.

46 Reed, "Leadership Surveys Church Conflict."